MACMILLA

INTERMED

DAVID NICHOLLS

One Day

Retold by F H Cornish

Founding Editor: John Milne

The Macmillan Readers provide a choice of enjoyable reading materials for learners of English. The series is published at six levels – Starter, Beginner, Elementary, Pre-intermediate, Intermediate and Upper.

Level Control

Information, structure and vocabulary are controlled to suit the students' ability at each level.

The number of words at each level:

Starter	about 300 basic words
Beginner	about 600 basic words
Elementary	about 1100 basic words
Pre-intermediate	about 1400 basic words
Intermediate	about 1600 basic words
Upper	about 2200 basic words

Vocabulary

Some difficult words and phrases in this book are important for understanding the story. Some of these words are explained in the story, some are shown in the pictures and others are marked with a number like this: ...³. Phrases are marked with ᴾ. Words with a number are explained in the Glossary at the end of the book and phrases are explained on t~~he Useful Phrases pages.~~

Answer Keys

Answer Keys ~~f~~ ....ctions
can be found a ....

Contents

A Note About The Author

David Nicholls was born in Hampshire, in the south of England, in 1966. When he was at comprehensive school[1] he wanted to be a doctor, then an actor, a drummer, a scientist and an artist. He finally decided to be an actor and he studied English and Drama at the University of Bristol. After that he went to New York, where he continued his training as an actor.

He returned to London in 1991 and worked as a waiter in restaurants and bars before he began his professional acting career. He worked at the West Yorkshire Playhouse theatre and at the Royal National Theatre in London.

After ten years of acting David Nicholls began to write. He worked as a scriptwriter[2] in the radio drama department of the British Broadcasting Corporation (BBC) and later he wrote television dramas too. He wrote original plays and also TV versions of classic novels. He has continued to write scripts, as well as the novels for which he has become well known.

David Nicholls's first novel, *Starter for Ten*, was published in 2003 and was a great success. Three years later the book was made into a film, the script of which was also written by David Nicholls. *Starter for Ten* was followed by *The Understudy* (2005) and *One Day*, which was published in 2009.

David Nicholls lives in London with his partner[3] and two children.

A Note About The Story

In one of William Shakespeare's plays, a character says that everything he has heard about love tells him this – that 'the course of true love never did run smooth'. He means that love between two people is never easy – there are always problems to overcome[4]. These problems have to be overcome before a couple can be happy together. Things always go wrong before they go right and people can finally marry. This is the subject of all Shakespeare's comedies. It's also the subject of *One Day*. David Nicholls's novel is about the problems in the 'course of true love' between two people – Dexter Mayhew and Emma Morley.

The word group 'one day' can be used in several ways in English. In the sentence 'One day, something strange happened', the words refer to a known date in the past and a real event. In the sentence 'One day, something wonderful will happen', they refer to an *un*known date in the future and to an event you hope will happen. And you can also say something like 'One day of the year (or month, or week) is always especially important to me.'

The main meaning of the title of David Nicholls's book is this third kind of meaning. Each chapter in the book is about what happens to one or both of the two main characters on one single day – 15th July – of a particular year. Chapters 1–17 are about the lives of Dexter and Emma during the years 1988–2004. Chapter 18 is about the events of 15th July in 2005–2007. And the final chapter, Chapter 19, is about 15th July 1988 again – the same day we read about in the first chapter. In some years, Dexter and Emma are together on 15th July. In other years, their only contact[5] on that date is a telephone call, an answerphone message or a letter. And in a few chapters, they have no contact at all on that date, for various reasons.

The other two uses of the words 'one day' are important in the book too. This is because the memories and hopes of the novel's two main characters are an important part of what we read about.

There is a kind of novel which is sometimes called 'picaresque'. It has been a favourite kind of writing for many British authors of the last sixty years. Picaresque novels are usually written in many separate episodes[6]. And they are often about badly behaved young men who do not really deserve[7] the women who love them. However, life is usually good to them by the end of the story. These novels often tell us about the social life of the time when their stories happen, as well as about their main characters. Some of Kingsley Amis's famous early novels, from the 1950s, are of this type. And David Nicholls's *One Day* is this kind of novel too. It is a love story which also tells us about how some young people lived their lives in the late twentieth and the early twenty-first centuries.

One Day is an international best seller and has been translated into many languages. David Nicholls has also written the screenplay for the film version, which was released in 2011. The film stars Anne Hathaway as Emma and Jim Sturgess as Dexter. The director is Lone Scherfig.

1

The Future

Friday, 15ᵗʰ July 1988
Rankeillor Street, Edinburgh, Scotland

'The important thing in life is to make a difference – to make a change to something,' the girl said.

'Ah – you mean we have to change the world?' the boy replied.

'No, not *all* of the world, we just have to change the bit of it around us,' the girl said. She was silent for a moment, then she laughed at herself. 'I can't believe I said that. It's such a predictable[8] thing to say, isn't it? But what *are* you going to do with your life? What's your plan?'

'Well, my parents are coming to collect me later today,' he told her. 'Then I'll go to France for a few weeks and after that, maybe I'll go to China.'

'Oh, you're going *travelling*,' she said wearily[9]. 'You're predictable too. You've got too much money, that's your problem, Dexter. What you really mean is that you're running away from real life.'

'Travelling broadens the mind[P], Emma,' he said slowly. He was trying to copy the girl's accent. Suddenly, he leaned over her and kissed her.

'I think you're too broad-minded now,' the girl said, quickly turning her face away from him.

The girl was from Yorkshire, in the north of England. She was used to posh[10] boys from the south making fun of her soft northern accent. Sometimes she didn't care, but now she

7

suddenly felt annoyed[11] with the boy. Everything was going wrong tonight. 'Anyway, I'm not talking about the immediate future,' she told him. 'I'm not asking about tomorrow, I'm asking what you want to be in twenty years from now.'

At first, the best answer he could think of was 'I want to be rich and famous'. But then he thought a bit more and spoke seriously. 'I don't ever want to be different from this,' he said. 'I'd like to stay exactly as I am now. Every fifteenth of July, I want to be just like this.'

The girl was called Emma Morley. The boy's name was Dexter Mayhew. They were lying on the narrow bed in Emma's room in a shared flat. It was four o'clock in the morning. The two young people didn't know each other very well, but certainly this was a night for thinking about the future. It was the last night of their university life in Edinburgh. Earlier in the day, after four years, they had finally graduated[12]. Soon they would go in separate directions.

Emma looked up at the boy as he leaned over her. She was a little annoyed with him, but she still thought that he was handsome. 'Mm – handsome. Perhaps "beautiful" is a better word,' she thought. And she knew that lots of the other girl students agreed with her – especially the posh ones from the south. They all knew that he would get their clothes off and get them into his bed. His body was muscular and the skin of his face was tight. His eyebrows were slim and his lips were full. 'Yes, he's beautiful, but he looks a little like a cat,' Emma told herself.

'I think I can imagine you when you're forty,' she said unkindly. 'You'll have an expensive red sports car and live in the most expensive part of London. You'll be married to your third wife – no, I'm wrong, your *fourth* wife. There won't be any children. You're too selfish[13] for children. No children, just three expensive divorces[14].'

'Well, Em,' Dexter began crossly[15].

'Who's "Em"?' Emma quickly asked.

'Your friends call you "Em", I've heard them call you that,' he said.

'Ah, yes, my *friends* call me that,' Emma replied.

'Can't I call you that?' he asked. He sounded worried.

'Oh, all right then, *Dex*,' she said. 'Go on.'

'Well, if you think I'm so terrible why are you sleeping with me?' he asked.

'Well, I don't think I really have slept with you, have I?' she replied. 'You can choose either meaning of "sleep" – I mean, we haven't been to sleep and we haven't done anything else, have we?'

'No,' the boy said, 'no, we haven't quite done that.'

Tonight Emma had wanted something different. She wasn't sure what it was, but their names sounded good together. 'Emma and Dexter,' she thought. 'Em and Dex.'

'Wait there,' Emma said. 'I'm just going to the bathroom. Don't go away.' She put on her thick glasses and walked towards the door.

In the bathroom, Emma asked herself why she was being difficult with the boy. 'He's certainly very bourgeois[16] and he isn't very clever, but I really like him,' she told herself.

Emma had liked Dexter since she'd first met him at a party two years before. But she'd never got to know him and in just a few hours he would be gone. And he certainly wasn't going to ask her to go to China with him. It was a bit sad. For the first time in four years she was with a boy she really liked. But she couldn't relax with him. They had been kissing and talking for eight hours now and she still didn't know what she wanted.

Dexter, waiting in the bedroom, looked around him. He had been in so many rooms like this one – rooms where girls like Emma lived. These girls always wore t-shirts with political slogans[17] on the fronts. There were always political posters on their walls. There were always CDs of political songs. They

were all the same, these girls with socialist[18] ideas. They always
thought that *he* was horribly bourgeois and they always thought
that being bourgeois was bad. Well, he had news for them. He
thought that being bourgeois was just fine.

Dexter hadn't really decided yet on a map for his future life.
But he was twenty-three years old and he had *some* ambitions[19].
He wanted to be successful at something – he just didn't know
at *what*. He wanted to make his parents proud of him. He
wanted to meet lots of women. He wanted to have lots of fun
in his life and he wanted never to be sad.

Thinking about fun and sadness, Dexter was now feeling
that this night had been a mistake. There were going to be
tears. There were going to be angry phone calls.

Emma returned and lay down beside him again. She had
put on a t-shirt with a political slogan on the front.

'Do you mind if we just cuddle[20], Dex?' Emma said.

Dexter didn't think this was a good idea at all, but he didn't
say so. 'OK, if that's what you want,' he said, without interest.

'I can't believe I just said "cuddle",' Emma said, after a
minute of silence. 'What a terrible bourgeois word for me to
use! I'm sorry.'

'We must get some sleep,' said Dexter. He was thinking,
'This must never happen again.'

———

There was daylight outside the window. Dexter was still awake
and he was looking at Emma, who was sleeping next to him. 'I
could leave quietly now, before she wakes up,' he told himself.
'Then I don't need to see her again. Will she mind? Probably,
girls usually do mind. But will *I* mind?'

It was strange, but the answer to this was not clear to
Dexter. There was something about Emma. She was pretty, but
she seemed to hate herself for that. The red colour of her hair
was out of a bottle and her hairstyle was awful. Dexter guessed
that Emma's hair had been cut by Tilly Killick, the large, noisy

'Do you mind if we just cuddle, Dex?' Emma said. Dexter didn't think this was a good idea at all, but he didn't say so.

girl who lived in the other room in this flat. 'But never mind the hair,' Dexter thought. 'Her face is really pretty and her body's *amazing*.'

Soon he decided that he *would* leave quietly, never mind what Emma's face and body were like. 'I'll probably never see her again,' he told himself.

Dexter was about to get quietly out of bed when Emma woke up.

'What are you doing later today?' she asked, sleepily.

'Tell her you're busy!' said a voice in Dexter's head.

'I don't have any plans,' he said aloud.

'Shall we do something together then?' she asked.

'Yes, all right,' Dexter said.

A moment later, Emma was asleep again.

2

Real Life

Saturday, 15ᵗʰ July 1989
Wolverhampton, England and Rome, Italy

E mma Morley was writing a letter.

Stoke Park School, Wolverhampton

Hello Dexter,

How are you? How is Rome? How is La Dolce Vita? *(Try a dictionary!) I know that some people call Rome 'the eternal[21] city' but I've been here in Wolverhampton for two days now and they have felt eternal to me. So perhaps Wolverhampton should be called by that name. Ha ha.*

Well, I decided to take the job I told you about, so I'm working with Sledgehammer Theatre. It's a Theatre-in-Education group. For the past month, we've been touring schools with a play about slavery[22]. Today we're performing it at this fine school. Anyway, we try to show 11–13-year olds that slavery was A BAD THING. Aren't we brave and original!

Really, I don't know why I am being nasty[23] about my job. A lot of the kids have never thought about social problems of the past until now. And now some of them – the ones that don't throw things at us – are becoming really interested. So I still think that we can make a difference for people.

Emma was trying to be positive. She had to try hard. The last year had been full of mistakes.

After her graduation, she had stayed on in Edinburgh. But she had made a series of bad career choices. There was the

13

terrible all-girl band she had played in. There was her first novel, which she had stopped writing. There was her second novel, which she had also stopped writing. She had worked in shops, trying to sell things to tourists. But the tourists never really wanted the things she tried to sell them. So finally she had moved back to Yorkshire to live with her parents. That wasn't good either.

'But you've got a really good degree,' Emma's mother said almost daily. 'Why on earth[P] don't you use it to get yourself a good job?'

From time to time, Dexter Mayhew became part of her life for a few days. At the end of the summer, she had gone to stay at his rich parents' huge house in the countryside. But that had gone terribly wrong. Emma had had too much to drink one evening and had argued with Dexter's father about politics. She had shouted at him and told him he was a bourgeois fascist[24]. Then, more recently, they had met up in London for the birthday party of one of their friends – a man called Callum O'Neill. Callum had shared a flat with Dexter in Edinburgh. He now had a successful business selling computers.

Dexter and Emma had spent the day after the party together. Most of the day they lay on the grass in Kensington Gardens. They drank wine from a bottle and they talked. They never quite touched each other and Dexter told her all about a wonderful Spanish girl called Lola. Emma decided that this was all their friendship was ever going to be. Clearly, Dexter didn't want to sleep with her. He wanted to tell her about the other girls he slept with. But strangely, Dexter also told her that his mother had liked her very much. 'She says she has a good feeling about you and me,' he'd said. At the time, Emma hadn't understood the importance of Dexter's words. Emma didn't know that Dexter loved his mother more than anyone in the world. And she didn't know that Dexter's mother felt the same about him.

Then Dexter had gone travelling again. When he was away, Emma wrote him long letters. He usually replied on postcards.

'We're just pen pals now,' Emma told herself. 'We'll never be anything more to each other.'

Emma got a job in a pub for a while, but living with her parents was killing her mind. When an old friend phoned and offered her a job in his theatre group, she'd accepted it immediately. But now, after three months, Emma hated the theatre group.

'I don't want to be here making a difference,' she thought. 'I want to be in Rome. I want to be with Dexter Mayhew.'

Emma made herself continue with her letter.

Anyway, I've got a new plan. I've written a two-woman play about Virginia Woolf and Emily Dickinson. One of my friends from the theatre group and I want to find somewhere in London where we can stage it. Do you remember my friend Tilly Killick? We shared a flat in Edinburgh. She lives in London now and she has a spare room in her flat. So I'll probably live there for a few months. Are you coming back to London soon? Maybe we could be flatmates?

Emma stopped writing. Suddenly she felt nervous. Then she wrote: *It's all right, I'm just joking! But I* really *miss you, Dex.* And she signed her name.

———

In Rome, Dexter was out with a Danish girl. He was working as an English teacher and the girl was one of his students. She was nineteen.

'I have an exam on Monday,' the girl said. 'Test me on verbs, please, Dexter.'

'All right – the present continuous,' Dexter replied.

'I am kissing, you are kissing, he is kissing ...' said the girl. She showed him how to kiss too. 'But what would Emma Morley think about this?' Dexter suddenly thought.

15

3

The Taj Mahal

'Listen to me, please, everybody,' Scott McKenzie shouted. 'The restaurant opens in ten minutes and I have a few things to tell you.'

Scott was the manager[25] of Loco Caliente, a Tex-Mex[26] restaurant in Camden Town, North London. The restaurant was one of a chain[27].

'First, these are the special dishes for this lunchtime,' Scott went on when his staff had stopped talking. 'Today's special soup is corn chowder[28].'

Several of the waiters pretended[29] to be sick and he stopped talking again for a few seconds. 'And today's other special dish is "an amazing fish burrito[30]" which contains "delicious pieces of cod and prawns". That's how the document from headquarters describes it, anyway – and those are the words you must use too.'

'It sounds really horrible,' said one of the waiters, laughing.

'Look at it this way – we're bringing a taste of the North Atlantic to the beaches of Mexico,' said Emma Morley. She sounded very tired as she made the joke. As she tied her waitress's apron round her waist she noticed someone she hadn't seen before – a large man with curly, blonde hair. He was wearing a waiter's uniform and he was quite nice-looking.

'And now here's some good news at last,' said Scott. He pointed at the stranger. 'This is Ian Whitehead, who is joining our happy team. Ian – this is Emma. She'll look after you today. She's been here longer than all the others.'

'This is Ian Whitehead, who is joining our happy team.
Ian – this is Emma. She'll look after you today.'

Emma did not think that this was anything to be proud of. She gave Ian a little smile as one of the waiters turned on the lunchtime music. The first song was, of course, 'La Cucaracha'[31]. She asked herself once more what she was doing here. She asked herself once more what she was going to do with her life.

Later, when Emma was showing Ian what he should do, she asked him about himself.

'I need to be in London,' he said. 'I took this job because I need to earn some money on the side[P].'

'Why? What do you really do?' Emma asked.

'Well ...' he said, in a funny accent, 'really, I'm a comedian!'

'A comedian! What kind of comedian?' asked Emma.

'I do stand-up comedy[32] in the evenings. I do gigs[33] at small comedy clubs, but they don't pay me very much.'

Then he surprised her. He asked her to go on a date[P] with him that evening – to one of the clubs. She was touched[34], but she refused.

———

In Bombay, Dexter Mayhew was writing a letter.

Emma, Emma, Emma. How are you? What are you doing? I'm in Bombay and it's raining. It rains here even harder than it rains in Edinburgh. It's too wet to go out so I'm staying in my hotel room. I'm a bit drunk, are you surprised?

I've seen some amazing things here in India and I've taken thousands of photos. I'll show all of them to you very, very slowly when I get back. I showed some of them to a TV producer[35] I met a few days ago. She's from London but she's making a film here. I think she liked me – she wants me to call her when I get back to England. Maybe she'll have a job for me in TV! I'll need to work soon and I'm banned[36] from teaching English to foreigners. I'm not sorry about that, I hated it. But I was treated very badly. That Danish girl was twenty-one!

What are you doing now? Are you still sharing a flat with Tilly? Are you still working at that horrible restaurant? You need to leave that job, Emma. Listen to me, Emma! We need to do something about your life. I'm drunk at the moment, so I'm just going to tell you what I think. You are clever. And you are beautiful. And you are loveable. And you are SEXY! You should be CONFIDENT! I want to take you away from boring people like Tilly Killick and Callum O'Neill, the computer king. Would you like to live with me when I get back to England? We would just be flatmates, of course.

Now, here's my plan to change your life. Are you sitting down? The shock might knock you over! You should be here with me in India. I'm going to wire you some money[P]*. I've always wanted to wire someone some money – it will make me feel important. Use the money to buy a plane ticket to Delhi. Then take a train to Agra and go to the Taj Mahal. Have you heard of it? It's a big white building and it's named after that Indian restaurant on the Lothian Road in Edinburgh. Be there exactly at noon on 1ˢᵗ August. Stand under the dome with a red rose in your hand. I'll find you. I'll be carrying a white rose. Isn't that the greatest plan you've ever heard in your life?*

Well, Emma, I'm still drunk, but it's stopped raining. I'm going out now to meet some Dutch people in a bar. I met them earlier today. They're all girls. They're nice. Don't forget – the Taj Mahal at noon on 1ˢᵗ August. I'll find you.

After he had finished the letter, Dexter took a cold shower and soon he was feeling better. He was almost sober[37] now. As he was dressing, he saw the letter, lying on his bed. Should he send it? Suddenly he felt nervous. He'd called Emma clever and beautiful. He'd called her loveable. He'd called her sexy! He'd asked her to live with him. Would she be angry with him? Would she come to India? Did he really want to see her that much? He decided that he did. He decided that he would post the letter that evening. He put it in his pocket and he went out. Then he walked happily to the bar where his new friends were waiting.

——

At about nine o'clock that evening Dexter left the bar with one of his Dutch friends – her name was Renee. As they left, they bumped into a large German girl with a huge backpack. She was a student from Cologne and she was called Heidi. She was tired and cross, and she swore[38] quietly at Dexter – it had been a long day. She crossed the room and sat down heavily on the sofa where Dexter had been sitting. A few minutes later she moved sideways across the sofa and felt something hard pressing into her leg. She swore again. There was an envelope between the cushions of the sofa. She pulled it out and looked at it.

Heidi opened the envelope and took out the letter. She read it to the end. Her English wasn't very good, but she understood most of the letter. She realized that it was important. It was the kind of letter she wanted someone to write to her. It was a beautiful letter. She wanted this person called Emma to receive it. But there was no name written on the envelope. And there was no address written on the letter. What could she do? Sadly, she realized there was nothing she could do.

4

A Career Opportunity

'Listen to me, please, everyone,' Scott McKenzie shouted. 'The restaurant opens in ten minutes and I have some things to tell you. First, these are the special dishes for this lunchtime.' Scott stopped, looked around him and then went on when his staff had stopped talking. 'Today's special soup is corn chowder. And the special burrito is turkey.'

'Turkey's not a good idea in July,' said Ian Whitehead wearily. 'Turkey's really for Christmas.' He shook his head in despair[39]. This made Emma Morley laugh. Ian was now Emma's best friend, but she rarely laughed at what he said. Scott looked at the two of them.

'Ian, you can clean the toilets today,' Scott said. 'Emma, I need to talk to you in my office.'

Emma followed the manager into his office and sat down.

'I'll come straight to the point[P],' Scott said. 'I'm leaving Loco Caliente soon. I'm going to be the manager of a big, new restaurant in West London. Do you want to be the manager here when I go? It's a good career opportunity. Head office wants someone who isn't going anywhere. Someone who won't go away travelling or leave suddenly to start a more exciting job.'

And suddenly, Emma was crying.

'What's wrong, Emma?' Scott asked. 'Has somebody upset[40] you?'

'No, it's all right, Scott. It's really nothing,' Emma told him. 'Don't worry, I'll be fine in a minute.'

'Go and rest in the staffroom,' said Scott kindly. 'Give me your answer about the job tomorrow.'

A few minutes later Emma was alone in the staffroom. She looked around her in despair. She knew that she couldn't leave her job. She had to spend all her money on rent, so she needed to take the manager's job. But she didn't want to be a restaurant manager all her life. She still wanted to be a writer, or perhaps a film-maker, or a painter. She wanted to be *something* in the arts. She spent lots of time writing – she mostly wrote poems these days. But nothing was working well for her. Nobody wanted to publish[41] her poems. Emma knew that her mother was still trying to find jobs for her in Yorkshire. Some days, she thought she would go back there. 'I've had a battle with London and London has won,' she told herself. But she wasn't ready to stop fighting yet. She needed to be in London.

Emma opened her handbag and took out her special notebook. The book had a beautiful cover and lovely, thick, white paper. It was where Emma wrote her poems. Now she took out her best pen. She thought for minute, then she started to write a new poem about how she felt. The poem she wrote was quite short and she knew it was really bad. She turned back through the pages of the book and found an earlier poem called *Daybreak in Edinburgh*. She read it.

> *We lie here in the*
> *Narrow bed and talk*
> *About the future. I*
> *Look at him and think*
> *'Handsome' – stupid word – and I*
> *Ask myself the*
> *Hardest question,*
> *'Might it be the real*
> *Thing, this time?'*
>
> *Outside the birds begin to sing and*
> *Sunlight warms the curtain.*

Emma looked carefully at what she had written. 'Can I really make the bad things in my life seem better by writing about them?' she wondered[42]. She had just decided that she could *not* do that because that poem was rubbish too, when Ian came into the staffroom. Ian looked angry and unhappy.

'Emma,' he said, 'your friend is in the restaurant again – the handsome one. He wants to see you. He's with a girl – a different one this time.' Ian had seen several of Dexter's girlfriends. Dexter obviously liked to show them to Emma and this clearly upset her. It upset Ian too.

'He's a monster[43], Emma,' Ian said.

'No, he's not a monster, he's just an idiot[44].' Emma sighed[45] and went out into the restaurant.

Dexter was with a tall, thin girl with black hair and expensive black clothes. They were reading the menu aloud to each other and laughing about it.

'Hello, Emma!' Dexter said when he saw her. 'This is Naomi. Will you have a drink with us?' His voice told Emma that he was drunk.

'I can't do that, Dex, I'm working,' Emma replied. 'Goodbye.' She turned away and walked back to the staffroom. Later, before leaving the restaurant, Dexter left a handwritten note on his table.

———

Later in the day, after Emma had finished work, she found Dexter lying on the grass on Primrose Hill, a mile away. The evening sun was warm and he was almost asleep. A half-empty wine bottle told her the reason. Emma kicked his leg.

'Don't do that to me, Dexter,' she said angrily. 'Don't bring people into the restaurant to laugh at me. If you ever do that again, it's the end of our friendship.'

'I'm sorry, Em,' Dexter said. 'I'm really sorry. I apologize.'

Emma looked at him and decided that he meant what he said – for now. She sat down beside him.

'Won't your girlfriend be angry if she finds out that you left a note asking me to meet you?' she asked.

'Oh, Naomi isn't really my girlfriend,' Dexter replied happily. 'She's just someone I go out with sometimes.'

'I'm sorry, then,' said Emma. 'Clearly, I don't mean girlfriend, I mean victim[46].' She spoke sadly. And she thought, 'Em and Dex, Dex and Em. No, it's never going to happen now.'

She picked up the bottle of wine and drank from it. Dexter looked at her and he felt warm inside. He often thought that Emma Morley was the best person he'd ever known. But he'd never really told her that. And he didn't tell her that now. For some reason, he couldn't make himself tell her that.

5

The Rules

Dexter and Emma were lying sleepily on the deck of a small ferry[47]. The two friends were travelling from the Greek island of Rhodes to a smaller island. They were going to stay there for a week and they were both feeling happy.

Life was changing for them. After a year as manager at Loco Caliente, Emma had left her job. In September she was going to start a college course. She was going to train to be a schoolteacher.

And Dexter had a job now. He was working for a television company. He'd started with small responsibilities[48] – making the tea, doing research[49] for producers. But now he was working as an interviewer. He interviewed pop stars and actors on a programme called *The Bigger Picture*. He had a posh flat in Belsize Park – an expensive part of north London. He wore expensive designer clothes. And he had a new girlfriend, his fourth one after Naomi. She was a beautiful and successful model.

Emma didn't really enjoy Dexter's television appearances, but she always watched them. For *The Bigger Picture*, Dexter had invented a new character for himself. He was a 'man of the people'. When he interviewed pop stars and actors, he spoke with a cockney[50] accent. Emma had never enjoyed Dexter's version of a Yorkshire accent and she thought that his 'cockney' voice was even worse. Emma liked Dexter to know that she wasn't impressed[51] by his television career. She told him this often.

But all that was back in London. Today they were happy. Today, they were on a ferry among the beautiful Greek islands. They were on holiday together.

It had been surprisingly easy to arrange this trip. Dexter's girlfriend was very self-confident, so she had no problems about his holiday with another woman. And Emma occasionally slept with people but still didn't have a regular boyfriend. So they had made their plans together and they had decided on some rules of behaviour for the holiday.

> *The Rules:*
> *One: Separate bedrooms.*
> *Two: No flirting[52].*
> *Three: No sleeping together.*
> *Four: No nudity[53].*
> *Five: No board games[54].*

Emma had decided on the first four rules. Dexter had fought back with Rule Five. Emma enjoyed playing board games, but Dexter hated them.

The Rules had to be obeyed[55], Emma told herself now, lying sleepily on the deck of the ferry. The Rules made this holiday possible. But Emma wondered if Dexter was going to be able to obey them. And she wondered if *she* was going to be able to obey them.

They were half asleep when they heard an English voice.

'It's him,' said a man. 'He's on TV on Fridays.'

'Oh, yes,' said a girl. 'He's called Dexter something. You *are* that man who's on TV, aren't you?' She was speaking to Dexter now. And he was wide awake.

'Yep. On 'oliday, are ya?' said Dexter in his pretend-cockney accent.

'Yeah,' said the girl.

Dexter continued talking to her and didn't take any notice of the man. The girl was clearly impressed.

26

'Dexter, why do you speak like that?' Emma asked when the couple had gone. 'You aren't a Londoner and you went to Winchester College.'

'The TV viewers won't connect[56] with me if I don't seem like them,' Dexter explained. 'Not many of our viewers went to Winchester.'

'That's a very bad reason,' said Emma. 'And you've broken Rule Two already. You were flirting with that girl.'

———

Emma was sitting at a table outside a small café on the island and drinking coffee. Dexter had gone to find them somewhere to stay. 'Don't forget, we need *two* rooms,' Emma had shouted after him as he set off. And he'd looked back at her and shouted, 'Of course we do!'

'She looks so lovely these days,' he told himself. 'It's the contact lenses. I hated those thick glasses she used to wear. But now she looks great. These rules aren't going to make life easy.'

But an hour later, when he returned to the café, Dexter seemed very pleased.

'There's some bad news, Emma,' he said. 'I could only find one room on the island. It's a *wonderful* room, but it only has one bed. But it's a very large bed.'

Emma believed that Dexter hadn't *tried* to find two rooms. She believed that Dexter had never *meant* to find two rooms. And of course, she was correct.

'All right, let's go and see the room,' Emma said wearily.

But when they got there, Emma loved the room. The bed *was* a large one. And there was a balcony. They could stand on it and look out over the sea.

'The room is fine, Dexter,' Emma said. 'We'll stay here. And you'll stay on your own side of the bed, won't you?'

———

Late that evening, Dexter and Emma walked down to the beach. The sun had disappeared and no one else was there.

'Shall we swim, Emma?' Dexter said. By now, Emma could read Dexter's mind. She could almost hear it working. This wasn't difficult, because Dexter only thought about a small number of things.

'We don't have swimsuits with us,' Emma replied very slowly, speaking in the way people speak to young children.

'We don't *need* swimsuits. There's no one here,' Dexter said.

'I understand you too well, Dex,' Emma said. 'You just want to get my clothes off, don't you?'

Dexter was silent.

'You swim if you want to, Dexter,' Emma went on. 'I'm not going to show my body to the world. And you've forgotten Rule Four.'

A moment later, Dexter had taken off all his clothes and was running into the sea. Emma suddenly felt stupid. 'Why can't I be free and uncomplicated[57] like Dexter?' she asked herself. 'Why do I care who sees me?' She quickly took off her own clothes and she too ran naked into the sea. Soon she was standing next to her friend. He turned to face her.

'Can we talk about Rule Three, Em?' Dexter said gently. 'You see, I really want you.'

For a moment, Emma felt wonderful. He had said it at last. And it was going to happen, here and now, in the beautiful warm sea. Dex and Em, Em and Dex. It was going to happen. And then Dexter said the wrong thing. 'Of course, it isn't personal. I want nearly every woman that I meet,' he added. 'That's my problem. I can't escape it. It's like a nightmare!'

'Oh, poor Dexter,' Emma said angrily. 'I feel really sorry for you.' She was angry with Dexter and she was angry with herself. 'You're a stupid, stupid woman,' she told herself. 'You're stupid for thinking that he really cared about you.'

But a moment later, it was Dexter who was angry. He was looking over Emma's shoulder at the beach. A boy was stealing his clothes.

'Stop! Don't do that!' Dexter shouted. He started to run towards the beach. 'Those trousers cost me two hundred pounds!' he shouted at Emma, who was laughing.

When they reached the beach, the boy, and Dexter's expensive clothes, had disappeared. He hadn't taken Emma's clothes.

When she had stopped laughing, Emma got dressed and Dexter found a torn, blue, plastic bag on the beach. He held this in front of him as they ran back to their room. On the way, they passed the English couple they had met on the ferry.

'I like the bag,' the man said. 'It's a great colour.' He laughed mockingly[58]. Dexter didn't reply.

But when they got back to their room, Dexter's anger had gone. It was a beautiful evening. And soon, the stars were bright in the sky. He and Emma had some food, then they got into the bed and lay in the dark. They didn't touch each other, and they knew that their friendship was unchanged.

'Tell me a secret, Em,' Dexter said. 'Tell me something about yourself that I don't know.'

'Well, I don't want to make you more arrogant[59] than you already are,' Emma replied. 'But here's something you didn't know. Before I first talked to you, when we were students, I was in love with you. And I used to write poems about you.'

'That was *before* you knew me,' Dexter said. 'Aren't you in love with me now?'

'Oh, *now* – things are quite different *now*,' said Emma.

When she said that, Dexter started thinking about his own secrets. He'd never told Emma that he'd once slept with Tilly Killick. It had happened when he was visiting the flat Emma and Tilly shared. Emma had gone out to the shops for an hour. He was never going to tell her about that. He didn't know that Emma knew about it already and it wasn't a secret at all.

'Tell me about those poems,' Dexter said quietly, after a few minutes. 'What rhymed with Dexter?'

'Monster,' Emma replied quickly. 'It's a half-rhyme.'

'Em,' Dexter said a few minutes later, 'how many rules did I break today?'

'Three,' Emma said. 'You broke Rules One, Two and Four.'

'And we nearly broke Rule Three,' Dexter thought. 'But we have eight more days. Anything can happen in eight days.'

'Well, at least we didn't play any board games,' he said aloud.

Emma was asleep.

PART TWO – THEIR LATE TWENTIES

6

Poison[60]

Thursday, 15th July 1993
Belsize Park, London and Oxfordshire

Dexter Mayhew was sitting in his flat in Belsize Park. It was 10am and Dexter was very drunk. He had been drinking all night with some new friends.

Now that he worked in television, lots of people wanted to know Dexter. They all wanted to hear his stories about the famous people that he interviewed. They all wanted to drink with him. So he was often drunk these days. Usually, being drunk in the mornings didn't matter. Dexter worked in the afternoons and evenings and he was always sober by then. But this morning, the morning of 15th July, it mattered very much. Today he had to go to his parents' house in the country, in Oxfordshire. He was already late. He knew, in part of his mind, that he *wanted* to be late. In fact, in that part of his mind, he didn't want to go at all. Because today, thinking about his parents made him want to scream.

Dexter's mother, at forty-nine, was fifteen years younger than his father. Dexter liked his father and they usually got on well together. But his feelings about his mother were quite different. Dexter loved his mother more than anyone in the world. But now his mother was dying and Dexter knew that she couldn't live much longer.

He needed to see her, but he was afraid. He was afraid to see how close to death she was. So this morning, he needed to be strong. He needed to make himself drive to his childhood[61] home. And he needed to make himself behave normally when he got there.

Dexter looked at the large parcel, wrapped[62] in brightly coloured paper, which he'd put next to his front door. He'd put it there so that he wouldn't forget it when he went out, even if he was drunk. The parcel was a present for his mother from his good friend Emma Morley.

Emma and his mother were very different people, but when they had met they had always enjoyed each other's company. And Stephen and Alison Mayhew had guessed that Emma was a good friend to their son. They hadn't really been offended[63] at all when Emma called Stephen 'a bourgeois fascist'.

Remembering this, for a moment Dexter wanted to phone Emma. The two of them had still never touched each other, but he knew that she was his best friend. Suddenly, he wanted to tell her that she was a dear, wonderful person. And he wanted to tell her how unhappy he was about his mother's terrible illness. But he knew what Emma would say. 'She'll know I'm drunk as soon as I start to speak,' he told himself. 'She'll tell me that I mustn't drive.'

Dexter picked up his car keys and collected Emma's parcel. He locked the door of his flat behind him and walked to his expensive, green sports car.

———

An hour later, Dexter was still worrying about his dying mother. But he also knew that he was lucky to be alive himself. He had fallen asleep for a moment and had almost crashed his car into a big truck. He could still hear the noise of the truck's horn in his aching head. He wasn't far from his parents' house now, but he had to stop for a while. He slowed down and drove into a pub cark park. It was a pub which he had often visited when he was young. He bought a glass of vodka and a glass of beer and sat down. He drank quickly and soon he was feeling better.

He walked outside into the sunlight and got into his car. In less than twenty minutes, he parked in front of his parents' house, just as his father opened the front door.

'I'd hoped you were coming earlier,' his father said as Dexter got out of the car. He looked angry and when Dexter tried to kiss him on the cheeks, he moved quickly away. At the television studios[64], everyone kissed everyone else on the cheeks. Dexter had forgotten for a moment that his father lived in a different world.

'Your mother hoped you were coming earlier too,' Stephen Mayhew added. He looked carefully at his son, then he sighed deeply.

'I'm sorry – I'm so sorry,' Dexter said unhappily. 'How is she, Dad?'

'You need to ask her that yourself,' Mr Mayhew said. 'Go up to her room now. I'll make us some lunch.'

Dexter walked slowly up the stairs, carrying Emma's present. He opened the door of his mother's bedroom and went nervously inside. Alison Mayhew was sitting up in her bed. She was very thin and she looked very tired and ill. But she smiled when she saw her son.

'A present! What have you brought me?' she asked.

'The present is from Emma,' Dexter said. 'Let's open it.'

The parcel contained books – long, serious books – Edith Wharton, Scott Fitzgerald, Raymond Chandler.

'How kind she is,' Alison Mayhew said. 'I'm very grateful to Emma. But please suggest to her that short stories might be more useful in future.'

Dexter tried to laugh, but inside his head he was screaming.

A few minutes later, he went downstairs to the kitchen, where his father was making lunch. Dexter picked up a glass of wine and drank it quickly, then he refilled the glass.

'Dexter, please be careful,' his father said. 'You drink too much. Alcohol is poison for you these days.'

33

'Your mother hoped you were coming earlier too,'
Stephen Mayhew added, then he sighed deeply.

'I've got a headache, Dad,' Dexter said. 'I've been working too hard. I'm going to lie down for half an hour. I don't need any food.'

He went upstairs to the room he had slept in when he was a child. A few minutes later he was unconscious[65] on his childhood bed.

———

It was evening when Dexter woke. The whole afternoon had passed. He went to find his father in the kitchen.

'I'm sorry, Dad,' he said. 'I didn't mean to sleep that long. Why didn't you wake me?'

'It wasn't my job. You're not a child any longer, Dexter,' his father replied angrily. 'And you were so drunk, there wasn't any point in waking you. You don't think that your mother wanted to see you like this, do you?'

'I'm sorry,' Dexter said again. He looked around the room. 'Where did I put my car keys? I have to go now.'

'I've got them and I'm going to keep them,' his father replied. 'You must *not* drive when you're drunk, Dexter. You'll kill yourself or you'll kill someone else, which will be worse. I'll drive you to the station now. You can get the train back to London. And you can come and collect your car at the weekend, if you're sober by then. Perhaps you'll be able to talk sensibly to your mother then, too.'

Dexter tried to argue, but his father wouldn't listen to him. And he wouldn't talk to him on the way to the station. But as Dexter was getting out of the car, the older man held his arm.

'Listen to me, Dexter,' Stephen Mayhew said very seriously. 'Your mother was looking forward to your visit today. And now she's very upset. She hasn't long to live, you must know that. If you come here drunk again, I won't let you into the house to see her. Do you understand me? I won't open the door to you.'

Stephen drove away and Dexter walked sadly into the station. When he was waiting for the train he tried to phone

Emma. 'Emma will understand me,' he told himself. 'I need to see Emma.' But Emma wasn't at home. He left a message on her answerphone. He asked if they could meet later that evening. He said he'd call again.

When he got back to his flat and called again, Dexter still got the answerphone. 'Emma, where are you?' he said to the machine. 'I miss you. I need you. I'll try again later.'

Covent Garden and King's Cross, London.

Emma didn't get any of Dexter's phone messages that evening because she wasn't at home. When Dexter left his first message, she had just left her flat in Earls Court, West London. She was walking to the nearby Underground station. She was on her way to an Italian restaurant in Covent Garden where she was going to meet Ian Whitehead.

Emma had only seen Ian a few times since she had left Loco Caliente to train as a teacher, but they were still friends. They sometimes talked on the phone. And tonight he had invited her to meet him for dinner. They had been friends for three years, but Emma had never slept with Ian. She knew that he wanted to sleep with her. She liked him, but did she want to sleep with him too? She didn't know and she wondered now how the evening was going to end.

At the station, Emma bought a ticket and waited for her train. Soon, it arrived and Emma boarded it. She sat and thought about how her life had changed since she had met Ian. She no longer shared a flat with Tilly Killick. Now she lived on her own in the small rented flat in Earls Court. And now she was ready for a new career. Tomorrow she was going to an interview for a job as a teacher of English and Drama. The job was in a comprehensive school in Leytonstone, in a poor part of East London. Emma was very confident about this job. She had enjoyed her year at teacher training college and she knew that she was going to be a brilliant teacher.

Yes, her life had changed. But Emma knew that her character had changed too. She had mellowed[66]. She no longer had a strong opinion about everything that happened in the world. Sometimes, she could even see that there were two sides to any argument.

'I'm twenty-seven – perhaps that's the reason,' she thought. 'Perhaps I'm getting old. Perhaps I'm ready to compromise[67].'

———

When Emma arrived at the restaurant, she saw that Ian was already there. She hoped that this was the beginning of a pleasant evening. Later, she'd decide about what was going to happen next. They ordered food and wine and Ian started to talk. He seemed very nervous and Emma tried to help him to relax.

But an hour later – at about the time Dexter was leaving his second message on her answerphone – Emma was feeling desperate[68]. Ian had been trying much too hard to make her laugh. She guessed that he was practising his stand-up comedy act on her. The problem was that everything he said was a joke and it was impossible to have a conversation with him. This was driving her crazy. She guessed that Ian was feeling desperate too. Everything he said made the evening worse. In part of her mind Emma wanted to leave and go home. But in another part of her mind she felt terribly sorry for Ian. It was clear to her that he wasn't a good comedian and that his ambition to have a career in stand-up was just a dream.

At last, she couldn't listen to any more bad jokes.

'Ian,' she said suddenly, 'will you be quiet for a minute, please! Will you just shut up[69]!'

Ian looked very surprised and he stopped talking. After a few minutes of silence, he asked quietly, 'Do you see your friend Dexter much these days?'

Emma suddenly understood why Ian had been so nervous all evening.

'No, we don't meet very often,' she replied. 'But we speak on the phone most days. He's busy with his TV career and his girlfriends – you know what Dexter's like. He's always been a bit crazy and now he's a bit *more* crazy, I think. His mother is seriously ill and he's drinking far too much.'

'I'm sorry to hear that,' said Ian. Then, after a pause, he said, 'To be honest I never liked him much. I always thought that he took you for granted[P].' They were both silent for a few minutes. Then Ian spoke again.

'Well, we've finished the wine,' he said. 'Shall we have some brandy?'

––––––

By the time they left the restaurant, Emma and Ian were both a bit drunk. Outside the restaurant, Emma turned to Ian and kissed him. She had decided that tonight, she was ready to compromise.

'Shall I come home with you?' she asked quietly.

'Emma, that's a lovely idea,' Ian told her.

And when Dexter phoned Emma's number again at midnight, there still wasn't anyone at home. Emma was at Ian Whitehead's and she was going to stay there until morning. Dexter was now feeling desperate. So he called another number.

'Hi, Naomi, this is Dexter,' he said in his television voice. 'I miss you, girl. I need you tonight. Can you find a taxi and come to my flat?

7

Show Business

Emma Morley got up early on 15th July. Emma now lived in a rented flat in Leytonstone. It was quite near Cromwell Road Comprehensive School, where she taught English and Drama. She had moved to the flat when she started teaching at the school, in the autumn of the year before. Ian Whitehead spent much of his time at the flat too. Emma thought she was probably in love with Ian. 'I *am* in love with him, aren't I?' she asked herself daily. And every day she told herself that she *was* in love with him – yes, of course she was in love with him. And her parents liked him very much, especially her mother. That was important to her. 'It's good when people's partners and mothers get on well,' she thought. But Ian did take up a lot of space in the little flat.

But Emma had a bigger problem than the size of her flat. Ian Whitehead and Dexter Mayhew – the two men in her life – still *didn't* get on well. Dexter didn't like Emma's friendship with Ian even though he had his own girlfriends. The truth was that Dexter needed Emma as an emotional support[70] but Ian didn't really understand this need. And Emma was especially important to Dexter now that his mother had died. Ian was also very jealous of Dexter, because he didn't want Emma to have a best friend who wasn't himself.

All this was a special problem on the 15th, because when the evening came, Emma was really needed in three places at once. Tonight was going to be Dexter's big night. Tonight, a new programme was going to be on television and Dexter was one of the presenters. This programme – *Late at Night* – was a much more important one than *The Bigger Picture* and perhaps it was going to make Dexter a big star. Another of the presenters – a glamorous woman called Suki Meadows – was already a star.

The programme was going to be live[71] and Dexter wanted Emma to be at the television studio to support him. He no longer saw his other friends from university. He no longer *wanted* to see them. Callum O'Neill, whose computer business was doing well, often called. He left messages on Dexter's answerphone but Dexter never called him back. Emma was the only one of his old friends that he cared about.

But tonight was going to be Emma's big night too. Emma was in charge of[P] her school's end-of-year drama production, the musical[72] *Oliver!* And the performance[73] was happening tonight. Of course this wasn't as important as Dexter's programme, but clearly Emma had to be there. She'd spent many weeks preparing the children for the show and she had to be with them. Tonight their parents were coming to watch them. And for their parents, they were all going to be little stars, for one night at least. Emma hoped it was going to make her the headmaster's little star too. Her teaching career – making a difference – was just as important as Dexter's more glamorous TV career, she thought. She knew that Dexter didn't really believe this.

And then there was Ian. Ian was feeling ill today. He didn't really want to go out at all tonight. And he didn't want *her* to go out. But she understood. She loved him, didn't she? And he *was* going to come to *Oliver!*, even if he still felt ill. He'd promised her that.

Before leaving to go to work Emma picked up the phone and called Dexter's number. She got his answerphone. 'Hi! Speak to me! Leave me a message!' Dexter's 'cockney' voice said on the recording. So she left him a message.

40

'Hi Dex, I'm sorry it's early for you,' she said. 'You're probably not awake yet. But some of us have jobs to go to. I'm sorry I won't be with you at the studio tonight, but I want to wish you luck. I know you understand that it's my big night too. That's show business, Dex! I'll speak to you later. Lots of love to you. Oh – and Dex – you really have to change that answerphone message.'

———

Dexter Mayhew wasn't feeling good when he arrived at the television studio on the Isle of Dogs. It was his father's fault. His father had left a message on his answerphone earlier in the day.

'I called to wish you luck for tonight,' his father had said. 'I'll be watching the programme. It's so sad that your mother isn't here to see you. She was so … proud of you. Well, good luck Dexter. And don't take any notice of the newspapers.'

When he'd heard the message, Dexter had gone out and bought all the daily newspapers. He'd opened the first one at the television pages and read the headline.

IS DEXTER MAYHEW THE NASTIEST MAN ON TV?

Dexter had drunk some vodka to settle his nerves[P] as he read the story beneath the headline. The story wasn't kind to him. Dexter was a stupid, rich boy who'd been educated at Winchester College but pretended to be a cockney, the author wrote mockingly. Dexter thought that he was popular with young people, the author said, but really young people just laughed at him. They didn't connect with him at all. Dexter had felt sick when he read this. And he had had several more drinks before he arrived at the television studio that evening.

In his dressing room at the studio, Dexter sat quietly trying to relax. He had told the producer of the show that he wanted to be alone. He was nervous. He had been a TV presenter for several years now, so he was surprised at how nervous he

41

felt. He didn't know what he was going to say when the show started. When he thought about the whole hour the show was going to last, his mind was suddenly empty. Now, he was very frightened. And the show was going to start in a few minutes. He took a bottle of vodka from his overcoat pocket.

There was a bottle of water on a table in the dressing room. Presenters usually took a bottle of water onto the set[74] with them. The studio lights were always very hot and they often needed to drink some water when they were off-camera. They couldn't speak clearly if their mouths were dry. But Dexter wanted something to clear his mind, not something to wet his mouth. He emptied the water into his washbasin and refilled the bottle with vodka. Then he put it back on the table. It looked the same as before. Nobody would know that he was drinking vodka.

'HEY THERE!' said a loud voice. 'WELL, HOW ABOUT ALL THIS?'

The owner of the loud voice was Suki Meadows. Suki was already a popular presenter of late-night TV shows. Now she stood at the door smiling at Dexter. She was a small, pretty, friendly person and she was always cheerful. *Always!* It didn't matter what was happening around her. She was cheerful and she was noisy.

'Why does Suki always speak in capital letters?' Dexter had sometimes asked himself. But tonight he was thinking something else. 'The viewers all love her. And she *is* very sexy,' he was thinking. 'And I'm sure she's crazy about me.'

Suki was wearing a very short skirt and a shirt made of very thin cloth. And she was holding her own bottle of water. 'COME HERE, DEX,' she said, entering the dressing room. She put her water bottle on the table next to his and put her arms around him. 'YOU'RE GOING TO BE GREAT TONIGHT! WE'RE GOING TO BE GREAT TOGETHER! DEX AND SUKI, SUKI AND DEX! WHAT A TEAM, DEX!'

And having wished him good luck in her own way, Suki led Dexter out of the dressing room. On the way, they picked up their water bottles. Outside, on the set, they picked up their microphones and inserted their earpieces[75]. They looked around them at the brightly coloured set and the brightly dressed dancers who were standing ready to begin the warm-up[76] before the show.

Then the music started, the dancers danced. When they had finished, Suki walked to the front of the set and yelled to the audience.

'ARE YOU READY TO HAVE A GREAT TIME? WELL, MAKE SOME NOISE FOR US!'

At that moment, Dexter realized that he was hopelessly drunk. Now it was his turn to speak and he couldn't say anything. He didn't know what to say. This show was going to be a disaster[77]. Someone in the audience shouted, 'You useless idiot! Can't you speak?'

Dexter had an idea. 'Well, *he's* clearly been reading the newspapers,' he shouted to the audience. He tried to laugh. A few of the audience laughed too, but not many of them.

Dexter needed another drink to clear his head, he told himself. He took the top off his water bottle and drank. It was water, just water. At once he understood. The bottles had got mixed up. Suki had the vodka. And she was taking the top off her bottle. He wanted to stop her drinking, but it was too late. As she tasted the liquid, Dexter saw the shock in her eyes.

And at that moment, the live programme began.

'We're live! Say something Dexter,' the producer's voice said in his earpiece. But Dexter *couldn't* speak and Suki was coughing. She recovered first, and she came to Dexter's rescue. 'SORRY ABOUT THAT. BUT AT LEAST YOU VIEWERS KNOW THAT THE PROGRAMME IS LIVE!' she said.

Suki went on speaking. Dexter tried hard to think clearly and after a few minutes he was able to perform better with

Suki. He wasn't very good, but he wasn't terrible. And Suki was amazing. She always spoke when Dexter didn't know what to say and she tried to make Dexter look normal. The show wasn't a disaster.

_____

When the programme had finished, there was a party for all the people who had appeared in it, and their friends and relations. Dexter stayed for the party, but he was quiet and thoughtful. People congratulated him, but they didn't speak to him for long. He ate lots of food and drank lots of wine, but he wasn't happy. He knew that he hadn't performed well. He knew that Suki Meadows had rescued him. And he knew that she had been the star.

Late in the evening, Suki came to sit next to him.

'That went OK, didn't it?' she said. For the first time that day, she wasn't speaking in capital letters.

'You saved us, Suki,' he said. 'I was trying to settle my nerves, but I drank too much before the show. I owe you an apology^P.'

'Yes, you do,' she replied. 'You have a problem with alcohol and we need to talk about it. You must understand this, Dexter – you won't appear on this programme with me again if you aren't sober. And you must never bring alcohol onto the set again.'

'What can I do to make you feel better about me?' Dexter asked her.

'Well, you can take me out for dinner next week,' Suki said. 'Take me somewhere very expensive. On Tuesday.'

Dexter thought for a moment. He had promised to meet Emma on Tuesday evening, but he could change that. Emma was his best friend. She was always there for him.

'All right,' he replied. 'We have a date.'

'Good,' said Suki, kissing him. 'And now, you must come and meet my mother.'

Dexter was feeling a bit unhappy on the Isle of Dogs, but Emma was on top of the world[P] in Leytonstone. *Oliver!* had been a great success. Of course there had been arguments and fights among the children before the show. That always happened. They were excited and some of them were nervous. But Emma had settled their nerves and when the music began, they all worked together and helped each other. So the show had been wonderful. Phil Godalming, Emma's headteacher, was very pleased. People whose children could act and sing like that were going to be proud, he thought. They were going to speak well of the school – and of its headteacher, of course.

At the party after the show the school staff, and many of the proud parents of the cast, congratulated Emma. She drank her wine and smiled at everyone. And late in the evening, Mr Godalming came to sit next to her.

'You're a wonderful teacher, Emma,' he said quietly in her ear. 'And you look very beautiful tonight. I have great plans for you next year.'

8

A Crisis

Saturday, 15ᵗʰ July 1995
Walthamstow, East London and Soho, Central London

'I'm going out now, Ian,' Emma called. Then she added carefully, 'Are you *sure* that you don't want to come with me, darling? Dexter will be pleased to see you, if you do come.'

'No, I can't come tonight.' Ian replied, entering the room. 'I've got things to do tonight, don't you remember? I'm performing at the House of Ha Ha. You go on your own. I'll be fine.'

This was the right answer, Emma thought. She was quite glad that she was going to see Dexter alone. She wanted to talk to him about her relationship with Ian Whitehead.

Emma was beginning to understand that she had made a bad mistake about Ian. They were living together now in a flat in Walthamstow. They had bought the flat together. And that was the mistake. Ian loved her very much, Emma knew this. And she had told herself often that she really loved him too and that she wanted to spend her life with him. But she now knew that it wasn't true. She was no longer happy with Ian. She just didn't love him.

She knew that Ian hated the success of her career and that he hated the failure of his own career. He still wanted desperately to be a stand-up comedian, but he only ever performed at pubs and small comedy clubs. Ian just wasn't very good at stand-up and he didn't earn much money from it.

Emma was feeling trapped[78]. So she needed Dexter to understand. She hoped it was going to be possible to talk sensibly to him tonight. She was feeling a little nervous about

46

that. Perhaps talking about Ian wasn't going to be easy. In the past, it *had* been easy to talk to Dexter. But now he had changed. He drank far too much and he was more careless than ever about people's feelings.

Ian wasn't Emma's only problem of course. She was no longer enjoying her job much either. She was a good teacher, she knew that. But she got tired and she didn't have much time to write. She still wanted to be a writer, but when she did write, the results were never very good. That was as bad a problem as her relationship with Ian. But the greatest problem for Emma was that she knew, in her heart, that Dexter Mayhew was the person she really loved.

So there it was. Everything was a bit hopeless. Ian's career wasn't what he'd hoped for and her career wasn't what she'd hoped for. She had a feeling that Dexter's career wasn't quite what he'd hoped for either. Suki Meadows was his girlfriend these days. But *she* was now clearly the star presenter of *Late at Night*. Dex was definitely the number two person. He wasn't very popular with the audience. And nasty people often wrote cruel things about him in the newspapers now.

Emma and Dexter were meeting for dinner at an expensive restaurant in Soho. It was the kind of place where fashionable people ate – people in television, like Dexter and Suki Meadows. Emma hoped she was going to like it.

Dexter was waiting for Emma outside the restaurant. He was talking on his mobile phone. Emma heard his caller's voice quite clearly as she arrived.

'TEN MILLION VIEWERS THIS WEEK, DEX!' the voice said, very loudly. 'TEN MILLION!'

'Suki, let me explain something about telephones,' Dex replied into the phone. 'You don't need to shout into them. The phone does the shouting for you. I have to go now,' he added when he saw Emma. 'I'll see you soon.'

'Dex, those things are so stupid,' Emma said, pointing at Dexter's phone. 'Why don't you throw it away?'

'You'll have one in less than six months,' Dexter replied, kissing her. 'You'll see. I'm right.'

They went inside the restaurant and sat at the bar where Dexter bought drinks. After a few minutes, they heard a soft, female voice behind them.

'Do you want cigarettes, sir?' the voice said. They turned to see a very tall, extraordinarily beautiful girl. The girl was dressed only in black underwear and stockings[79], and she carried a tray containing the cigarettes. She had a fixed smile. It wasn't a happy smile. Dexter bought some cigarettes. He spent a long time finding his money, so that he could look at the girl's body. Then the girl moved away.

'Why is she dressed like that, Dexter?' Emma said.

'I don't know, Em,' Dexter replied. 'Perhaps all her ugly clothes are in the laundry. You could look like that if you wanted,' he added. 'You've got a great body.'

'But I don't want to look like that,' said Emma.

Soon a waiter took them to their table. They ordered drinks and when those arrived, they ordered food. Dexter was drinking quickly. 'And soon he'll be drunk – again,' Emma told herself. And she couldn't stop thinking about the cigarette girl. 'Why am I eating in the kind of restaurant where girls have to dress like that?' she asked herself. Then she asked Dexter the same question.

'This place is terrible, Dex,' Emma said. 'Haven't women made *any* progress in the last hundred years?'

'You don't understand, Em,' Dexter said. 'Dressing like that gives her power over men. She enjoys it.'

'Don't be stupid, Dexter,' Emma said. 'The owner of this place makes her wear those clothes. If she doesn't wear them, she'll lose her job. She only works here because she needs the money, you can see that. She has no power over anyone!'

'Well, you're still the same old Emma, aren't you?' Dexter said crossly. 'Emma, the angry, socialist feminist. I thought that you'd mellowed, but clearly I was wrong about that. You never want to compromise, do you?'

After that, the evening got worse and worse. Dexter frequently left the table to visit the toilet. Each time, he stopped to talk to the cigarette girl. The last time it happened, Emma saw him push a piece of paper into her stocking. Emma had no doubt that he was giving the girl his phone number.

When he returned to the table, Emma decided she had had enough of his behaviour. She pushed the table away from her, spilling their drinks, and ran up the stairs out of the restaurant. She could hear Dexter behind her, calling her name. She didn't turn round.

In the street, Dexter finally caught up with her.

'Emma, I'm sorry, I'm *sorry*. I didn't mean to upset you,' he said desperately.

Suddenly, Emma turned to face him.

'Dexter, whenever I see you now you're drunk,' she said. 'I haven't seen you sober for three years. I don't know you any longer. You're obnoxious[80] these days. You were always a *bit* obnoxious, but now you're *totally* obnoxious.'

'I'm just having fun, Emma,' Dexter replied.

'Well, it isn't fun for *me*,' Emma replied. 'Let's stop this now, Dexter. You don't care about me. We don't have to meet any more.'

'Emma, of course we have to meet,' Dexter said desperately. 'We're Dex and Em, aren't we? We'll *always* be Dex and Em.' For a moment he was quiet. He was thinking of the day of his mother's funeral. He was thinking of Emma's kindness to him that day. She had held him as he cried uncontrollably. He had always taken her for granted, he knew that. 'Why am I throwing all this away?' he was asking himself. But he knew that he couldn't stop himself.

'Dexter,' Emma said sadly. 'I love you very much and I probably always *will* love you. But I'm afraid I don't like you any longer. I don't like the person that you've become. I don't want to hear from you again. Please don't try to contact me.'

She left him standing in the street and walked away.

PART THREE – THEIR EARLY THIRTIES

9

Things End

Monday, 15th July 1996
Leytonstone and Walthamstow, East London

At six o'clock on the last day of term at Cromwell Road Comprehensive School, almost everyone had gone home. Only Emma Morley and Mr Godalming, the school's headteacher, were still in the building. They were lying on the floor of Mr Godalming's office.

'I'll miss you very much during the holidays, Emma,' Mr Godalming said as they put on their clothes. 'I'll miss our Friday afternoons together.'

'No you won't, Phil, you'll have Mrs Godalming,' Emma replied unkindly. 'You'll be fine.'

Emma wondered, as she spoke, why she always felt so cross after their meetings in the headteacher's office. Afterwards she always felt unhappy and that made her cross.

They collected their coats and books and the headteacher locked the office. As they walked to the school car park, Emma was thinking hard. She had been Phil Godalming's lover for nine months now and she was starting to worry about this. She was afraid that he was going to tell his wife about their relationship and ask for a divorce. That was not what Emma wanted at all. She didn't love Phil. She had never really loved him. For a short time, he had made her feel better when her life had become very sad. She wasn't seeing Dexter any longer and she missed him. And her relationship with Ian Whitehead had gone wrong. Phil had helped her to be confident during the bad times. But she certainly didn't want to marry him. And she thought now that it was time for this relationship to end.

As Mr Godalming opened the door of his car, Emma held his arm.

'Phil, I'm sorry but I don't want to be your lover any longer,' she said. 'I feel bad about our relationship. I feel bad about your wife. I'm not happy.'

'You were very happy ten minutes ago, Emma,' the headteacher said. He laughed.

'No, Phil, *you* were very happy ten minutes ago,' Emma replied sadly.

Phil Godalming wasn't pleased to hear Emma's words. He'd enjoyed their meetings after school on Fridays. He argued for some time, but clearly, Emma wasn't going to change her mind.

'We'll talk about this next term,' he said. He got into his car, closed the door and drove quickly out of the car park.

Emma travelled sadly home to Walthamstow on the Underground. On her way home, she bought some wine to drink later. She was going to spend the evening on her own. Ian Whitehead no longer lived with her. They had ended their relationship after a terrible argument. They had argued about Ian's jealousy and his selfishness. At the end of their argument they had both cried. They had cried for each other and for the end of their relationship. But they both knew that it had to end. It had all been so sad, Emma thought now, as she sat in the train.

———

Late that evening, after she had drunk the wine, Emma turned on her television. The first person she saw was Dexter Mayhew. Suddenly, Emma realized that it was exactly a year since she had spoken to him. She knew that Dexter's TV career hadn't been very successful recently. Viewers had never really loved him, it seemed. They had only loved to hate him. And nowadays most of them just hated him. Dexter was now presenting a very late-night TV show about computer games. Few people watched it.

Emma did watch the show for a few minutes. She thought that Dexter wasn't looking well. His face was looking tired and he no longer seemed confident. Suddenly, Emma had a great feeling of friendship and love for him. She realized that for the last eight years, she had thought about Dexter every day. Now she knew that she wanted his friendship again. She wanted him to be her *best* friend again.

'I'll call him tomorrow,' she told herself. 'I really will call him.'

10

Resignation[81]

Tuesday, 15th July 1997
Central London

The River Thames looked lovely on this warm, sunny afternoon, Emma Morley thought. It was a work day, but Emma wasn't at school. Teaching had finished for the term but there was a very important staff meeting happening at the school. Emma was needed there, but she didn't really care about that. She had phoned the headteacher's secretary that morning and told her that she was ill and had to stay in bed. The woman clearly hadn't believed her. Emma didn't care about that either.

Emma wasn't really ill at all. In fact, she was feeling good. And she *had* been to a meeting – a meeting with a publisher. At last Emma was feeling confident about something she had written – a novel for young readers. It was about a group of children at an East London school. The children were appearing in a school production of *Oliver!* and the story was told by one of the actors – a girl called Julie Criscoll. Julie was a rude, angry, teenage girl with a good heart[P]. The book was funny and touching. Emma had included silly drawings and handwritten pages in her text, so parts of it looked like a schoolgirl's diary. She knew that what she had written was really good. And now, other people thought it was good too. Perhaps soon, she was going to be a published author.

Emma wanted to write and she wanted even more to stop teaching. She thought every day about resigning. Her job at the school had been very difficult for the last year. Phil Godalming had been angry because she no longer wanted to sleep with him. He'd tried to make her life difficult all year. And now she knew that she could write well, Emma wanted to spend her life writing. At her meeting this morning, she had told the publisher about her ambitions. The publisher had been helpful. Emma's life was going to change.

As she walked by the river, her mobile phone rang. Emma *did* now have a mobile. Dexter had been right after all. Phil had given it to her during the months when they'd been close. 'I want to be able to hear your voice at any time,' he'd told her. As she took the phone from her handbag, Emma guessed that it was Phil phoning her now. She wasn't wrong.

'So, you're ill in bed, are you?' he said in his special loud, angry headteacher's voice. 'Well, I don't believe it. I think you're outside, enjoying the sunshine. I can hear the traffic noise.'

'Don't shout at me, Phil,' Emma said quietly.

'My name's Mr Godalming, not Phil,' the man replied. 'This is serious, you know that. I told you that today's meeting was a very important one. There'll be trouble about this, Emma. And if you don't want a relationship with me, I won't protect you from trouble. Your job is in danger.'

'No, it isn't,' Emma replied, laughing. 'I'm resigning from my job – now! Do you understand? I've resigned! Goodbye, Mr Godalming.'

She switched off her phone and for a moment, she thought about throwing it into the river. But after a few seconds, she put it back in her bag.

11

Dexter in Love

Wednesday, 15th July 1998
Chichester, Sussex

Dexter Mayhew was lying in bed with Sylvie Cope at the end of a difficult day. Recently, something strange had happened to Dexter. He had fallen in love. He'd had many lovers but he'd never been in love before. And now the girl beside him was more important to him than anything in the world. He almost couldn't believe his luck.

Sylvie was tall, slim and beautiful, with long, straight hair and a heart-shaped face. She and Dexter had known each other for several months and they spent lots of time together. Every weekend they flew to a different European city and they always had a wonderful time. They spent lots of Dexter's money in expensive shops. Sylvie was excited to know Dexter in real life, after seeing him on television. But the truth was that Dexter liked Sylvie much more than she liked him. But Dexter actually enjoyed this. It meant that Sylvie was different from his other girlfriends.

Sylvie worked in marketing[82]. Dexter had met many of her friends, who also worked in marketing. He hadn't liked them and they hadn't liked him. Who cared? And tonight, Dexter and Sylvie were staying at the home of her parents in Chichester. Today, Dexter had met the Cope family for the first time.

Dexter hadn't enjoyed meeting the Copes much. Sylvie's parents clearly didn't admire unimportant television presenters and Sylvie's twin younger brothers had mocked him openly.

But Dexter really didn't care about that. Sylvie was on his side^P and that was the only important thing. Sylvie was on his side and now she was by his side, in the big bed.

'I love you,' Dexter said to her quietly. He'd never said these simple words to anyone before. 'You're amazing!' he added. But Sylvie was already asleep.

As Dexter lay awake, he realized that he wanted to tell someone else about Sylvie and about his good luck. He wanted to tell someone he liked and trusted[83]. And suddenly, he knew who he wanted to tell. It was someone he hadn't spoken to for three years. He wanted to tell Emma Morley.

12

Weddings

It seemed to Emma Morley that all her friends were getting married this year. As she drove to Somerset, in the west of England, on the morning of 15ᵗʰ July, she thought of the weddings she had been to recently. Some of her friends from university had married for the first time that year. Some of them had married for the second time. Watching these wedding ceremonies had made Emma feel that she was growing old. All the university friends she met at them asked her if she had a boyfriend. And they all pretended to be sad for her when she said she hadn't. But they all said she was looking better than she had ever looked. They were right. She took better care of herself these days and she even wore pretty clothes for these occasions.

The best thing about these weddings for Emma was that she had met Dexter Mayhew at several of them. At last they were speaking to each other again, after more than three years of silence. That was very, very good. Of course, she had met Dexter's girlfriend Sylvie too and perhaps that was less good. But Dexter was clearly in love with the girl, so Emma tried to be happy for him. She had never seen Dexter really in love before.

This morning, Emma was driving to Somerset for the marriage of Tilly Killick. Tilly was getting married at a posh hotel in the countryside. Dexter had known Tilly during their university days too, so he was going to be there and Emma was looking forward to seeing him again. She was driving an old car. It was the first car she had ever owned and it was the best she was able to afford. Emma certainly wasn't a rich woman. In fact, she was now living on a small advance[84] from a publisher and was writing her second book about Julie Criscoll. But the first book was going to be published soon and the publisher expected it to sell very well.

Emma had some problems with her car during the journey and she was a bit late when she arrived at the hotel. The ceremony had already begun when she entered the big marriage room, so she found a seat at the back of the room. As she was sitting down, Dexter Mayhew turned round and saw her. He smiled and waved his hand.

Dexter was sitting at the front with Sylvie. He hadn't really been listening to the ceremony. He had been counting the number of women in the room he had slept with. 'It's five,' he thought. 'It's five in one room, including the bride. It's a good score. Is it a record? Do I get an extra point for the bride? And really, it's five-and-a-half if I count that night with Emma.' And as he thought this, he realized that it was a bad thing to think. He also realized that he wanted to talk to Emma very much. 'I'll try to talk to her alone,' he thought. 'I need to tell her everything.'

———

After the ceremony, the party began. Dexter left Sylvie with some friends and started to look for Emma. But the first person he met was Callum O'Neill. The two men hadn't spoken for a long time. Dexter had heard that Callum had sold his computer business for a huge amount of money. He had now started a new business – a successful chain of sandwich shops. Today, he was very expensively dressed in beautiful, fashionable clothes. Dexter remembered that at Edinburgh University, Callum had worn the same pair of trousers every day for three years. How things had changed! Callum had gone up in the world and Dexter had come down.

'Dexter, old friend, you're still alive,' Callum said. 'It's been a long time since I've seen *you*. I stopped phoning you because you never returned my calls.'

'Didn't I?' Dexter said. 'Well, you know, I've been very busy with my television programmes.' He tried to sound confident.

'And *are* you still on television? I haven't seen you on TV for a long time,' Callum said.

'I'm usually in programmes for sophisticated, late-night viewers,' Dexter said uncomfortably.

'Mm. Perhaps you need a new career opportunity,' Callum said. 'You could work for me, Dex. I need a new manager. Come and see me soon. I'll buy you a good lunch – not sandwiches. We'll talk about it. Now, let's go and find your lovely girlfriend. I saw you with her earlier and I want to meet her. Have you seen my girlfriend? I won't ask you to meet her, I'm getting rid of her[P] soon.'

———

Much later in the afternoon, Dexter finally met up with Emma.

'Let's go somewhere quiet,' he said. 'I want to talk to you.'

'Where's somewhere quiet?' Emma asked him.

'Well, there's a maze[85] here, I believe,' said Dexter. 'It's a large one. It would be nice to get lost in it.'

They found the entrance to the maze and they walked inside. They didn't stop until they reached the centre. Then they turned to face each other.

'Well, isn't it strange?' Emma began. 'These days, we only talk at other people's weddings.'

'I'm sorry that I've been so obnoxious during these last few years,' Dexter said quietly. 'I don't blame[86] you for ending our friendship. But I want us to be friends again now.'

'I'm sorry too, Dex,' Emma replied. 'Perhaps I didn't understand how badly your mother's death had hurt you. I didn't wait for you to start feeling better. We were both to blame.'

'I'm a different person now, Em,' Dexter said. 'Sylvie has changed me. I love her very much.' He stopped speaking for a moment. 'Emma, there's going to be another wedding soon,' he went on. 'Sylvie and I are going to get married later this year. And Sylvie is going to have a baby.'

For another moment they didn't speak, but their faces showed their real feelings. Then Emma knew that she had to say something to hide *her* feelings, at least.

'She's a lovely girl, Dex,' Emma said. 'It's marvellous news.'

'I think that fatherhood will transform[87] my life,' Dexter replied. 'I've almost stopped drinking already. I'll be a good family man.'

'Well, that's good,' said Emma. She laughed. 'Of course, you've just ruined[88] any chance of future happiness for me, but it's all great news.' She stopped for a moment. 'Don't worry,' she added. 'I'm only joking.' And then they both laughed.

'The wedding will be in September,' said Dexter. 'Emma, will you help me write my speech for the big day?'

'No, Dexter,' said Emma. 'Don't be an idiot. Just look into your heart and write.'

Then they walked back towards the entrance of the maze.

The Pleasures of Fatherhood

Saturday, 15ᵗʰ July 2000
Richmond, Surrey, England

Jasmine Alison Viola Mayhew – Dexter and Sylvie's daughter – had been born on the third day of the year. She was always going to be the same age as the century. Dexter loved her dearly. He wanted to do everything that was best for her.

After work on 15ᵗʰ July, he was hurrying home to the pretty house in Richmond where he and his wife and daughter lived. Richmond was ten miles west of London, so Dexter was no longer a Londoner. His flat in Belsize Park was rented to someone else.

Dexter really had almost given up alcohol. That was something he was proud of. He often felt pressure[89] to have just a small drink, but he rarely gave in to it. He *had* given in to pressure about something else. The pressure had come from Sylvie, who wanted him to find a real job. He had been getting very little TV work in the last year, so finally he agreed to have a meeting with Callum. Sylvie really liked Callum and Callum wanted to help them.

Callum had given Dexter a job. One day, it might become a very *good* job but at the moment Dexter wasn't enjoying it. The problem was that Dexter had to 'start at the bottom', as Callum said. He had to make sandwiches. He had to sell sandwiches in the shops. He had to drive a van around London. It was very menial work[90]. The worst thing about it was that he was frequently recognized by people. Customers in the shops often asked him why he was no longer on TV and that hurt him. He also worried that Sylvie was disappointed in him. She had pressured him about the job but he felt she was angry that his TV career had ended. He worried that she was no longer very interested in him. They often argued these days. And they hadn't made love for weeks.

Dexter was thinking about all this as he arrived home. But tonight he was going to prove to Sylvie that he *was* a new person. Tonight he was going to look after Jasmine alone while Sylvie went out with friends. It was going to be the first time Sylvie had left the baby for more than a few minutes.

'I'm going out for a meal in Central London with some of my girlfriends,' Sylvie had told him. 'Then we'll stay at a hotel overnight. I'll be back the next morning. It will be all right, you'll see.'

'Yes, it will be all right,' Dexter told himself now.

Sylvie looked tired and unhappy when Dexter entered the house.

'What's wrong, darling?' he asked her.

'Oh, it's just been a bad day,' she replied. 'Jasmine hasn't slept at all. She's been crying all day. And life in the house gets very boring when you aren't here. I'll feel better when I get out of the house tonight. Now, are you *sure* you'll be all right on your own with Jasmine?'

She tried to sound friendly, but Dexter knew that she didn't really trust him.

'She thinks I'll start drinking,' he told himself. 'But I will *not*! I will certainly *not*!'

'We'll be fine,' he said. 'Don't worry about us.'

'If there's a problem, call me,' Sylvie said. 'But call my mobile, *not* the hotel number. Do you understand?'

———

From the beginning, Dexter's evening was a disaster. Moments after Sylvie left the house, Jasmine started to scream and she didn't stop. She missed her mother. She didn't let Dexter feed her. Soon there was baby food all over her clothes and she was wet through. Dexter changed her clothes and laid her down, but she refused to go to sleep. Then she screamed when Dexter turned on the television and saw the face of Suki Meadows. Jasmine's scream was even louder than Suki's voice. Soon Dexter was desperate. And soon he was walking to the wine shop in the next street, with Jasmine in his arms.

When he returned home, Dexter opened one of the bottles of wine he had bought. As he drank, Jasmine finally went to sleep. Dexter began to feel calmer, but he didn't stop drinking. He looked at the baby food, the baby clothes and the baby toys that were all around him. He felt trapped. He drank some more wine. 'I need to talk to someone,' he told himself.

He tried to phone Emma Morley, but she didn't answer her phone. He waited for a few minutes and tried again. Still she didn't answer. Much later, and feeling desperate, he called Suki Meadows.

'Hi, Suki, it's me – Dex,' he said. 'I saw you on TV earlier. You were great.'

'DEX, HEY THERE! WELL, HOW ABOUT ALL THIS? I HAVEN'T HEARD FROM YOU FOR A LONG TIME,' Suki shouted. Suddenly she spoke quietly. 'In fact, it's been five years since we spoke.'

'Where are you, Suki?' Dexter asked her. 'I'd love to see you. There's so much to talk about. I want us to be friends again. Will you come to my house? Get a taxi – I'll pay for it.'

'I'm at a party with some friends,' Suki said, still speaking quietly. 'I'm not free. When we were together, you treated me really badly. Do you remember that? You can't just phone me after five years and tell me to come to you.'

At that moment, Jasmine woke up and started crying again.

'What was that noise?' Suki asked.

'It's a baby … it's my daughter, Jasmine,' Dexter said nervously. 'Didn't you know I had a daughter? I married someone and –'

He looked at the baby food, the baby clothes and the baby toys that were all around him. He felt trapped.

Suki said several very rude words and then ended the call suddenly. Dexter opened the other bottle.

———

Just before midnight, Sylvie used her mobile phone to call Dexter. She was sitting naked on the bed in her hotel room. They spoke for a few minutes, then Sylvie ended the conversation and began to cry.

'He was drunk,' she said to Callum O'Neill, who was sitting beside her. 'I knew he was going to be drunk.'

'Well, I've given him a job, there's nothing else I can do about him,' Callum said. 'The question is – what are *you* going to do about him? And when are you going to do it?' He turned on the television angrily and got into bed.

14

Another Man

Sunday, 15th July 2001
Paris, France

Emma was waiting at the Eurostar station in Paris. She was
waiting for Dexter to arrive on a train from London. She
was a bit nervous. They had only seen each other once since
his marriage to Sylvie had broken up[91]. On that occasion, they
had spent the night together. That night, she had finally slept
with him, for the first and only time. She thought now that
it had probably been a bad idea. But he had been desperately
unhappy and she had wanted to help him in some way. They'd
both been a bit drunk. Soon after, Emma had decided to get
away from England for a few months. She had come to Paris for
the spring and summer. She wanted to spend her time writing.
Her Julie Criscoll books were a great success and her publisher
wanted more.

Now Dexter was coming to visit her for a few days and she
hoped that they could both forget about that night and be
good friends again. But she had something to tell Dexter and
she was worried.

The train arrived and a few moments later Emma saw
Dexter walking towards her. He was carrying a book. He
looked terrible – he'd lost weight and his clothes were untidy
and too big for him. He looked desperately tired.

The end of his marriage to Sylvie had hurt Dexter a lot.
Their divorce was going to be made final soon. Sylvie and
Jasmine had now gone to live with Callum O'Neill. That had
made it worse for Dexter, of course.

'You didn't have to meet me,' Dexter said.

'Of course I had to meet you,' she said, smiling. 'You're a tourist.'

The two friends left the station and went to a café near the river. They sat down at a table outside it and Emma ordered coffee for them. Dexter put the book he had been carrying on the table. It was a copy of *Big Julie Criscoll Against the Whole World*.

'It's great, Em,' Dexter said. 'I read it on the train. I really enjoyed it. It's the first novel I've finished in years. There were hundreds of copies in the bookshop at the station in London. I'm really proud of you.'

'Well, thanks for that, but it's really a book for eleven-to fourteen-year olds,' Emma said. She laughed, but she was touched. 'The publisher wants two more Julie Criscoll books and there's going to be a TV show based on them too,' she went on. 'I'm going to be ...' She stopped when she saw Dexter's face and started to talk about something else.

They drank their coffee and then they walked through the busy streets to Emma's flat. As they walked, Dexter told Emma that he missed his daughter desperately. He saw her only once a fortnight[92], when Sylvie brought her to visit him.

Emma's flat was on the fifth floor of an old building. They climbed the stairs and Emma opened the door. The flat was light and pleasant. Emma went to the kitchen and Dexter looked into the other rooms. There was only one bed in the flat – a big one.

Dexter saw the bed, sighed deeply, then he hurried to the kitchen and put his arms round Emma. He started to kiss her wildly. But after a moment, she pushed him gently away.

'Dex, I have to tell you something,' Emma said. 'I've got a friend here in Paris. His name's Jean-Pierre. I like him very much.'

Suddenly Dexter understood. 'You're seeing another man?' he said. 'A *French* man? Oh, right. But where am I going to sleep? I need to find a hotel, don't I? Or shall I just go back to London this evening?'

'You can sleep here, Dex. I'll sleep at Jean-Pierre's flat,' Emma said. Dexter just looked at her. 'Oh, Dexter, what did you think was going to happen?'

'Well, we're lovers, aren't we? I hoped that you and I ...' He stopped. 'Oh, Emma, you can't ...'

'Dexter, you're *jealous*,' Emma said laughing. 'I can't believe it. This is so strange. We were lovers for one night! One night in thirteen years. Think of all the girlfriends you've brought to see me. You always told me who you were sleeping with. You didn't expect me to be jealous of them. And now ... and now ...' But she couldn't go on. She saw the pain and the hopelessness in his eyes. She put her arms round him and kissed him gently.

'Oh, Dexter,' she said quietly. 'I thought that I'd got rid of you. I thought that you weren't going to be my problem any more. All right, all right. I'll phone Jean-Pierre and tell him that I'm ill. But Dexter, if you ever treat me badly and go off with other people, I'll kill you. Do you understand?'

15

Monday Morning

Monday, 15th July 2002
Belsize Park, London

At seven o'clock in the morning, Dexter Mayhew and Emma Morley were lying awake in bed. They were thinking their own thoughts. They were now living together most of the time. Emma still kept her own flat, but at last they were close friends and lovers as well, and really, life was good for them both.

Emma's thoughts that morning were about the 15th July the previous year. She thought about that and about what had happened since then. Dexter's visit to Paris had been difficult at the start. But she had quickly realized that she hadn't really moved on[93] from him and that probably she wasn't able to move on from him. So she'd finished her relationship with her French boyfriend. Dexter had stayed with her in Paris for the whole summer and they'd returned to London as a couple. These days, Emma usually slept in Dexter's flat in Belsize Park and during the daytimes, she went to her own flat, two miles away. She rode there on her bicycle and wrote her books there. Emma's series of books about Julie Criscoll was selling very well. The television version of them was popular too, so Emma was almost rich now.

During the daytimes, Dexter now ran a successful delicatessen[94] and café in Highgate, another fashionable part of north London. Emma knew that he had hated doing menial jobs when he worked for Callum O'Neill. But now he seemed to enjoy doing the same jobs for himself. He enjoyed making the sandwiches and coffee for his customers at the deli.

Most of the time, Emma was confident about their future. She loved Dexter and she loved his daughter Jasmine, who often spent time with them. The three of them were happy together. This was good for Jasmine, because Sylvie and Callum were *not* getting on well together. But there was one little cloud in Emma's sky. She was beginning to wish for a child of her own. And she wasn't getting any younger, of course. Dexter already had a child and he wasn't so happy with the idea of another one. Sometimes they argued about this.

'Perhaps I need to find someone else,' Emma sometimes thought when this happened. But she never thought very seriously about leaving Dexter.

One day, Emma had met Dexter's father again. She remembered that meeting this morning.

'Of course I remember you, Emma,' Stephen Mayhew had said. 'You called me a bourgeois fascist once. I'm very pleased to meet you again.' And he'd told her, 'Dexter is so much better now that he has you with him. Suddenly, I like my own son again. It's wonderful.'

Now, as Emma stopped remembering things and started to get up, Dexter spoke.

'Why do you still keep your own flat, Emma?' he said. 'You can live here all the time. You know that.'

'Dexter, are you asking me to be your flatmate?' Emma replied, pretending to be surprised. 'It's taken you a lot of years, hasn't it?'

'Yes, I think I am,' Dexter said. 'And, yes it has. But that's what I want.'

'The flat's really too small, Dex,' Emma said after a few moments.

'Well, let's buy a house together, Em,' Dexter said.

71

16

bigdayspeech.doc

Tuesday, 15th July 2003
Yorkshire, England

'That's the place where I was bitten by a dog when I was a little girl,' Emma said. She pointed ahead. She and Dexter were walking along a beach on the Yorkshire coast. The morning was hot, but there weren't many people on the beach. The school holidays hadn't begun yet.

'What kind of dog was it?' Dexter asked. He was trying too hard to sound interested. Emma looked carefully at him. Clearly, he didn't really want to know what kind of dog had bitten her.

'Am I boring you, Dexter?' she asked. She sounded a bit cross.

'No, of course you aren't,' Dexter replied wearily. 'Well, perhaps you are boring me a little bit.'

'Ah, then you have four more days of boredom to look forward to, don't you?' Emma said. She laughed. She liked his sudden honesty. 'Poor Dexter,' she added.

Emma and Dexter were on holiday. They had rented a small cottage in the Yorkshire countryside for a week. Each day they set out to visit places that Emma remembered from when she was a child. Today, after their morning at the beach, they were going to drive inland. Emma wanted to find a waterfall she remembered from her childhood.

'It's a beautiful place, Dex,' she said. 'You'll love it.'

But that afternoon, they didn't succeed in their search. Emma's memory wasn't good enough. After an hour they hadn't found Emma's waterfall. So they found a pleasant spot in the sun and lay down on the grass. Soon, Dexter was feeling a bit sleepy.

'Look at that bird up there, Dex,' Emma said suddenly, pointing to the sky. 'What kind of bird is it? It's beautiful!'

Dexter did not look up. 'I'm too young to be a birdwatcher,' he said. 'Birdwatching is for middle-aged people. And isn't birdwatching a very *bourgeois* thing to do? Next, you'll want us to move to the country. Then you'll want us to cuddle in bed and call each other "darling" and go to the shops together.' For a moment, Emma thought about Ian Whitehead. Calling *him* 'darling' hadn't meant that she really loved him, had it? 'After that it's classical music – Beethoven and that kind of thing,' Dexter went on. 'I've seen it happen to people, Em. It's awful.'

Emma laughed and kissed him. 'It does sound awful. Tell me again – why *are* we going to get married?' she said.

'Well, we don't need to. We *could* cancel the wedding,' Dexter said.

'Yes, but we've paid for it now,' Emma said. 'Can we get our money back if we cancel it?'

'I don't think so,' Dexter replied.

'Ah well, we'd better get married then,' said Emma. 'I knew there was a reason.' And she kissed him again. Then she closed her eyes and thought about their wedding. They had chosen a day in November for the ceremony. Only a few close friends were going to be there. And finally she was going to be Emma Mayhew, after all these years. 'I'll marry you if you promise you'll never play golf,' she whispered.

———

That evening, they went to bed early. Emma quickly went to sleep, but Dexter couldn't sleep so he got up quietly and went downstairs.

He was thinking about Emma and about their big day in November. He was going to make a speech at the wedding party. He needed it to be just right. Suddenly, he remembered

73

something that Emma had once said to him. He turned on his laptop and opened a file. Then he looked into his heart and made some notes:

My wedding speech

1) I met Emma at University.
2) She called my dad a bourgeois fascist.
3) She can't cook.
4) We argue a lot – but laugh a lot too.
5) She's beautiful but she doesn't believe it.
6) She gets on well with my lovely daughter, Jasmine.
7) She even gets on well with my ex-wife. Ha, ha! *[Leave five seconds for laughter here.]*
8) Everyone loves her.
9) Our sudden romance lasted 15 years.
10) My wonderful mum loved Emma.

ALSO …

11) Say something nice about Dad and about Emma's parents.
12) Say that it's my second wedding and I need to get it right this time, etc.

He was reading what he had written when he heard Emma's footsteps on the stairs. He gave the file a name – bigdayspeech.doc – and closed it.

'Sorry, I fell asleep,' Emma said from the bottom of the stairs. 'But I'm awake now. What *shall* we do?'

'I think I'd like to play a board game,' said Dexter and he smiled.

17

Too Late

It was breakfast time in Belsize Park.

'Well, it didn't happen this month, Dex,' Emma said sadly. 'I'm sorry.'

'Please don't worry about it, Em,' Dexter said. 'We'll go on trying.'

'I'll be thirty-nine next April,' Emma replied. 'Soon it will be too late.'

Dexter now wanted a baby as much as she did. But it wasn't happening. They were both beginning to worry.

'It really doesn't matter,' Emma told herself. 'We're a happily married couple. That's the important thing. And Jasmine's here a lot.'

She told herself this, but there was a hole in her life now. It made her sad and sometimes it made her cross with Dexter for no real reason.

This morning she tried to be calm, but she was quickly upset by something in the newspaper.

'Dex, I don't understand students these days,' she said. 'They don't care about anything, do they? When I was a student, we protested[95] about things like this.'

She put the newspaper down in front of him and pointed at a story.

'Perhaps they're right not to protest,' said Dexter wearily. 'We aren't all socialist feminist anti-fascists, are we? Some of us have other things to worry about.'

And that started the argument. For ten minutes they were

very rude to each other. Then, quite suddenly, Emma didn't want to argue any longer.

'I'm sorry, Dexter,' she said. 'This isn't about students, is it? It's about not having a baby. I'm really upset about it. I don't want to fight with you.'

By the time they left the house they were almost friends again. Emma was going to her flat to write. Dexter was going to the deli, but he wasn't in a hurry. He now had help there. A pleasant girl called Maddy worked as his manager. And a few other people helped at busy times.

'There's a house that I want us to look at this afternoon,' Dexter said as they left the flat. 'We really must buy one soon and I've got a good feeling about this one. I'll phone you with the address later. It's in Kilburn. Meet me at the house at five o'clock.'

So Emma got on her bicycle and rode off to do her day's work. At about lunchtime, Dexter phoned with the address where they were going to meet.

'I'll see you there, darling,' Emma said. 'I'm sorry about this morning. I love you.'

———

At four o'clock, Emma set off from her flat to cycle to Kilburn. It started to rain and soon the roads were wet. There was lots of traffic noise. Emma didn't hear the car that came out of a side street at high speed. So she was surprised to be flying through the air.

She landed by the side of the road. When she opened her eyes, there were people standing round her.

'Are you all right, Miss?' one of them asked. Another was crying.

But Emma didn't speak. She knew that she was certainly *not* all right.

Two thoughts passed through her mind as she lay on the ground. One was a memory of herself playing on a Yorkshire beach. She was with her parents and she was nine years old. The other thought was about Dexter. She was going to be late for their meeting. He was going to worry and he was going to get wet. Then Emma Mayhew died and everything she had ever thought had gone.

18

Three Anniversaries[96]

Friday, 15th July 2005
London, England

The months had passed. A year had passed.

Very early in the morning of 15th July 2005, Dexter Mayhew was drinking in a club in Central London. It was the kind of club that stayed open very late. Dexter was alone. Earlier, he had come to the club with Maddy, his manager, and two of the other workers from his deli. Dexter had wanted them all to drink to the memory of Emma at exactly midnight, at the beginning of her anniversary day. They had gladly come with him. But soon after midnight the others had left the club. They needed to go home. Maddy had tried to make Dexter go home too, but he'd wanted to stay, and Maddy had left. Now Dexter was very drunk.

Finally, Dexter left and walked to another club, where he continued drinking. Soon he got into a fight. He knew that he wasn't going to win the fight. He didn't *want* to win the fight. He wanted to die.

The fight ended with Dexter lying unconscious in the street. When he woke, he found that someone had stolen his money and his keys. There was blood all over his clothes. Somehow, he found his way back to Belsize Park. But outside his front door, he realized that he couldn't get into the flat without his keys. He lay down and went to sleep on the ground. Sylvie found him unconscious there in the morning when she brought Jasmine for a visit.

Sylvie had ended her relationship with Callum O'Neill and Dexter now got on quite well with his ex-wife. When she found Dexter outside his door, she phoned his father. She had her own keys, so she took Dexter into the flat and washed him and found him some clean clothes. Later, Stephen Mayhew arrived and took Dexter back to Oxfordshire. Now that they had both lost their wives, they understood each other better. Dexter's father was gentle with him.

Saturday, 15th July 2006
London, England

The months had passed. Another year had passed.

For Dexter, the second anniversary of Emma's death wasn't as painful as the first one. When the deli closed for the day, he decided to spend the evening alone. He wanted to look through Emma's books and photographs. He was going to keep some of them. He was going to give some of them to her parents. The others were going to her friends.

So in the evening, he sat with Emma's things around him. He thought about the previous anniversary and he remembered a strange thing. A few days after 15th July last year, he'd received a kind letter from Ian Whitehead. 'When Emma left me, I hated you,' he had written. 'I wanted to die. But after a few years I met someone else and my life changed. And now I'm happy again. We have three children. I know how you must feel without Emma, Dexter. And I know that she loved you very, very much. I used to think that you weren't good enough for her. But none of us was good enough for Emma. And we have to go on for her. Please take care of yourself.'

After that letter, Dexter and Ian had spoken on the phone a few times. But they both knew that they weren't going to meet again.

Dexter spent a lot of the evening looking at Emma's old photos. He found some which Emma had taken on Arthur's

Seat[97] in Edinburgh. One of them had been taken by someone else and showed both Emma and Dexter. These photos had been taken on the first day they had ever spent together. Suddenly, Dexter felt terrible. There were so many memories. He started to cry, but he knew what to do. He phoned his friend Maddy. Talking to her made him calm again.

'Shall I come to you?' she said. 'I can get a taxi.'

'No, it's all right. I just wanted hear a friendly voice,' Dexter told her. 'I'll be fine now.' And soon, he felt much better.

Sunday, 15th July 2007
Edinburgh, Scotland

The months had passed. One more year had passed.

On the third anniversary of Emma's death, Dexter was in Edinburgh, with Maddy and Jasmine. Dexter and Maddy were a couple now and they were having a short holiday with Dexter's daughter. This morning, Maddy had told Dexter to take Jasmine for a walk. 'I'll go to one of the art galleries,' she'd said. She'd guessed that Dexter wanted to visit places from his past. She'd also guessed that he wanted to talk to Jasmine about Emma.

Jasmine was seven years old now and she walked happily beside Dexter. First they walked to Rankeillor Street and for a minute, Dexter looked up at the window of the flat where Emma used to live. Then they walked through the streets towards Arthur's Seat.

'Let's do some climbing,' said Dexter when they reached the hill. 'There's a wonderful view from the top.'

'Did Emma come up here too?' Jasmine asked him when they reached the top.

'Yes, we came here together,' Dexter replied. 'I have a photo of us both on the hill. I'll show you it when we get back to London.'

'Do you miss Emma?' Jasmine asked quietly.

'Yes, I miss her every day,' Dexter said. 'She was my best friend. Do *you* miss her?'

'I *think* I miss her,' Jasmine said. 'But I was only four when she died. I don't remember her very well. She was nice, wasn't she?'

'She was very nice,' Dexter said.

'Who's your best friend now, Daddy?' asked Jasmine.

'You are, of course,' Dexter replied quickly.

'Can we go down now?' Jasmine said. 'I'm a bit tired.'

19

The Past

Friday, 15th July 1988
Edinburgh, Scotland

Have you had someone in your room all night?' Tilly Killick asked, when Emma Morley entered the kitchen in their flat that morning.

'Oh, yes, it's only Dexter Mayhew,' Emma replied. She tried to sound uninterested. She was not very successful.

'It's *only* Dexter Mayhew! You lucky person,' Tilly said. She sounded a little jealous. 'Is he staying here all day too?'

'No, I think we'll go out after breakfast,' Emma said. 'What shall we do? Have you any ideas for a romantic[98] day, Tilly?'

'Well, Arthur's Seat is a good place to go, isn't it?' Tilly said. 'You can be romantic there.'

So after breakfast, Emma and Dexter went out into the city. Emma took her camera with her and they bought food for a picnic. Dexter was worried about climbing Arthur's Seat. He was wearing expensive shoes and he didn't want to ruin them.

'I don't climb mountains, Em,' he said. 'I'm not that kind of person.'

'Dexter, it's only a hill, it's not K2,' Emma replied, laughing.

So they climbed Arthur's Seat and when they reached the top they decided that it wasn't really romantic. There were too many people already there for that. But Dexter had never climbed the hill before and he was surprised. He enjoyed the view. It made an impression on him. This didn't often happen.

'I've lived in this city for four years,' he said. 'Now this is my last day in Edinburgh. Why haven't I been up here before?'

'Because you're not that kind of person,' Emma replied.

They ate their picnic and then they sat quietly together.

'Dexter,' Emma said after a few minutes, 'I want to say something. It's about last night. I haven't done that kind of thing often and I know that you were a bit drunk. I know it was just one night, and that's it. But I want to say that it was nice for me. It was nice and *you're* nice, Dexter. You're a nice person when you allow yourself to be nice. I really like you.'

Later, on their way back to the bottom of the hill, they stopped to take some photos. Someone took a photo of both of them together. Then Emma walked with Dexter back to his flat. They found Dexter's parents waiting for him there.

'This is my friend Emma Morley,' Dexter told his parents.

'Hello Emma, I'm Alison,' Dexter's mother said. 'We're pleased to meet you. Do you want to come for a drink with us?'

Emma looked at Dexter. He looked unhappy and worried. She made a quick decision.

'No, thank you,' she replied. 'That's very kind of you, but I have to get back to my flat.' Then she spoke to the boy. 'Have a nice life, Dexter,' she said quickly. She turned and walked away. 'I'll probably never see him again,' she told herself as she walked sadly along the street.

But a few minutes later, as she walked through the city centre, she heard someone call her name behind her. She turned and saw Dexter. He had been running and he was exhausted[99]. 'My parents came early,' he said. 'I didn't have time to get your address and phone number.' Quickly, Emma wrote these on a piece of paper and Dexter wrote his address and phone number for her.

'Call me when I get back from France,' he said. 'Come and stay with us for a few days. I want to see you again.'

Then he kissed her gently and she kissed him. They stood in the middle of the busy street and people on their way home hurried around them. It was the sweetest kiss either of them ever knew.

*They stood in the middle of the busy street. It was the
sweetest kiss either of them ever knew.*

'Goodbye, Dex,' Emma said.
'Goodbye.'
'Goodbye. Goodbye.'

Points for Understanding

PART ONE

1

1 Why was it 'a night for thinking about the future'?
2 What went wrong with Emma and Dexter's night together?
3 Emma and Dexter were very different from each other. List the differences.

2

1 Why was Emma unhappy in this chapter?
2 At the end of the chapter Emma decided to change her life for the better. What did she decide to do?
3 What were Emma's thoughts about Dexter in this chapter?

3

1 What did you learn about Ian Whitehead from this chapter?
2 How did Emma feel about her job at the restaurant?
3 How did Dexter try to help Emma in the letter he wrote to her when he was drunk?
4 What happened to Dexter's letter? Why was this sad?

4

1 Emma started crying when Scott offered her the job of manager. Why do you think she was upset?
2 What did Dexter do to upset Emma and make her angry with him?
3 What did Dexter really think about Emma? Why do you think he didn't tell her this?

5

1 In which ways had Dexter and Emma's lives changed in the past year?
2 Which of The Rules were broken on this holiday and when?
3 How did Dexter upset Emma? And why was she angry with herself?

PART TWO

6

1 Explain why Dexter, in part of his mind, didn't want to visit his parents.
2 Why did Dexter's father say, 'I won't open the door to you.'
3 Why didn't Emma get any of Dexter's phone messages that night?
4 Did Emma enjoy the meal? Give your reasons.

7

1 Why did Dexter want Emma to be at a television studio that night?
2 Emma couldn't go to Dexter's television show. Why not?
3 Emma's show was a success and Dexter's was a failure. Is this true? Why/Why not?

8

1 Emma's life was making her feel trapped. What were the reasons for this?
2 How did the girl selling cigarettes at the restaurant cause a problem between Dexter and Emma?
3 What was Emma's final reaction?

PART THREE
9

1   Emma was sad and alone at the end of this chapter. Give some reasons.

10

1   Why did Emma resign from her job?

11

1   What was unusual about Dexter's relationship with Sylvie?

12

1   Emma had been to a number of weddings. What did she think was 'the best thing about these weddings'?
2   What did we learn about Callum O'Neill, Dexter's university friend, from this chapter?
3   'For another moment they didn't speak, but their faces showed their real feelings.' What do you think this means?

13

1   How was Dexter going to prove to Sylvie that he was a 'new person'?
2   What did we learn about Sylvie that Dexter didn't know?

14

1   In this chapter, Emma's life was going well and Dexter's life was going badly. Explain why this is true for each of them.
2   What did Emma mean in the last paragraph of this chapter?

PART FOUR
15

1 '… and really, life was good for them both.' Give reasons why life was good for both Emma and Dexter now.

16

1 Emma and Dexter were going to get married but what 'middle-aged' things did Dexter *not* want to do? And what did Emma add to the list?
2 Why was it funny that Dexter said he wanted to play a board game?

17

1 Why did Emma and Dexter argue?

PART FIVE
18

1 What are the differences between the way Dexter felt and behaved on each anniversary?

19

1 What did Emma mean when she said, 'Have a nice life, Dexter'?
2 Do you think that it is true to say, 'It was the sweetest kiss either of them ever knew'? Give reasons for your answer.

Glossary

1 **comprehensive school** (page 4)
a UK school for students of different levels of ability between the ages of 11 and 18. A *comprehensive school* is paid for by the government and is often simply called a *comprehensive*. The main character, Emma, becomes a teacher in a school like this. The other main character, Dexter, went to Winchester College – a very old, traditional English public school – an expensive private school where students usually live as well as study. It was very different to the *comprehensive school* Emma teaches at, where there are students from poor families.

2 **scriptwriter** (page 4)
someone whose job is to write scripts – the written words – for films or television programmes

3 **partner** (page 4)
someone who you live with and have a sexual relationship with

4 **overcome** – *to overcome something* (page 5)
to succeed in dealing with or controlling a problem

5 **contact** (page 5)
communication between people, countries or organizations either by talking or writing

6 **episode** (page 6)
an event or set of events that forms part of a longer series but is considered separately

7 **deserve** – *to deserve something* (page 6)
If you *deserve* something, it is right that you get it, for example because of the way you have behaved.

8 **predictable** (page 7)
If something is *predictable*, it is not interesting because it happens a lot and people expect it.

9 **wearily** (page 7)
in a way that shows that you are tired or bored

10 **posh** (page 7)
Someone who is *posh* talks or behaves in a way that is typical of people from a high social class. This word often shows that you do not like people like this.

11 **annoyed** (page 8)
feeling a little angry or impatient

12 **graduated** – *to graduate* (page 8)
   to complete your studies at a university or college, usually by
   getting a *degree* – the qualification that you get after completing the
   course
13 **selfish** (page 8)
   thinking only about yourself and not caring about other people
14 **divorce** (page 8)
   a legal way of ending a marriage
15 **crossly** (page 8)
   in a slightly angry way
16 **bourgeois** (page 9)
   typical of middle-class people and their attitudes. This word often
   shows that you dislike people like this, especially because you think
   they are too interested in money and possessions and in being
   socially respected.
17 **slogan** (page 9)
   a short phrase that is easy to remember and is used to advertise
   something or to express the beliefs of a political party or other
   group
18 **socialist** (page 10)
   supporting a political system that aims to create a society in which
   everyone has equal opportunities and in which the most important
   industries are owned or controlled by the whole community
19 **ambition** (page 10)
   something that you very much want to do, usually something that is
   difficult to achieve
20 **cuddle** – *to cuddle* (page 10)
   if you *cuddle* someone, you put your arms round them and hold
   them close to show that you like or love them. Emma is saying that
   she does not want to have sex.
21 **eternal** (page 13)
   continuing for ever or for a very long time
22 **slavery** (page 13)
   the system of owning people as *slaves* – people who belong by law to
   another person as their property and have to obey them and work
   for them
23 **nasty** (page 13)
   unkind or unpleasant

24 *fascist* (page 14)
   an insulting word for someone who has very conservative opinions
   – for example, not being willing to accept change, especially in the
   traditional values of society
25 *manager* (page 16)
   someone whose job is to organize and control the work of a business
   or organization or a part of it
26 **Tex-Mex** (page 16)
   with a mixture of features from Texan and Mexican culture and
   cooking
27 *chain* (page 16)
   a group of businesses such as shops, hotels, or restaurants that all
   belong to the same person or company
28 *chowder* (page 16)
   a thick soup usually made with fish or shellfish, milk or cream and
   vegetables
29 *pretended* – *to pretend* (page 16)
   to behave in a particular way because you want someone to believe
   that something is true when it is not
30 *burrito* (page 16)
   a type of Mexican food made with a piece of flat thin bread called a
   tortilla that is folded over and filled with meat or beans and cheese
31 **La Cucaracha** (page 18)
   a traditional Spanish folk song that became popular during the
   Mexican revolution. It is very well known and is often played in
   the kind of restaurant Emma works in.
32 *stand-up comedy* (page 18)
   Ian is a *comedian* – someone whose job is to entertain people by
   telling jokes and stories to make them laugh. He does *stand-up
   comedy* – an activity in which one person stands in front of an
   audience and entertains them by telling jokes.
33 *gig* (page 18)
   a public appearance, especially to entertain people
34 *touched* (page 18)
   feeling happy or emotional, for example because someone has been
   very kind or because a situation is sad
35 *producer* (page 18)
   someone whose job is to organize the work and money involved in
   making a film, play, television programme, CD, etc. A person who
   introduces a television or radio programme is called a *presenter*.

36 **banned** – *to ban someone from doing something* (page 18)
to say officially that someone is not allowed to do something
37 **sober** (page 19)
not drunk
38 **swore** – *to swear* (page 20)
to use words that are deliberately offensive, for example because you
are angry with someone
39 **despair** (page 21)
the feeling that a situation is so bad that nothing you can do will
change it
40 **upset** – *to upset someone* (page 21)
to make someone feel sad, worried or angry
41 **publish** (page 22)
to produce many copies of a book, magazine or newspaper
42 **wondered** – *to wonder* (page 22)
to think about something because you want to know more facts or
details about it
43 **monster** (page 23)
someone who is very cruel
44 **idiot** (page 23)
someone who behaves in an extremely stupid way
45 **sighed** – *to sigh* (page 23)
to breathe out slowly making a long soft sound, especially because
you are disappointed, tired, annoyed or relaxed
46 **victim** (page 24)
someone who has suffered as a result of the actions or negative
attitudes of someone else or of people in general
47 **ferry** (page 25)
a boat that makes short regular journeys between two or more
places
48 **responsibility** (page 25)
a duty that you have to do because it is part of your job or position
49 **research** (page 25)
the detailed study of something in order to discover new facts
50 **cockney** (page 25)
a type of informal English that people – especially working-class
people – born in the eastern area of London called the East End
speak
51 **impressed** (page 25)
admiring someone or something very much, especially because of
an unusually good achievement, quality or skill

52 **flirting** – *to flirt with someone* (page 26)
to behave towards someone in a way that shows your sexual or romantic interest in them

53 **nudity** (page 26)
the condition of not wearing clothes, or of not covering a part of the body that is traditionally covered when you are in public

54 **board game** (page 26)
a game played on a board, often using dice and small pieces that are moved around

55 **obeyed** – *to obey something or someone* (page 26)
to do what a law or a person says that you must do

56 **connect** – *to connect with someone* (page 27)
to feel you understand someone or something and have the same ideas, opinions and beliefs

57 **uncomplicated** (page 28)
simple and easy to understand

58 **mockingly** (page 29)
If you *mock* someone, you make them look stupid by laughing at them, copying them or saying something that is not kind. The man speaks to Dexter *mockingly* – in a way that shows that he thinks he is stupid.

59 **arrogant** (page 29)
Someone who is *arrogant* thinks they are better or more important than other people and behaves in a way that is rude and too confident.

60 **poison** (page 31)
something that has a very negative effect on someone

61 **childhood** (page 31)
connected with the time in your life when you are a child. Your *childhood home* is the place where you lived when you were a child.

62 **wrapped** – *to wrap something* (page 32)
to cover something by putting something such as paper or cloth round it

63 **offended** (page 32)
upset and angry because of something that someone has said or done

64 **television studio** (page 33)
a room or rooms where a television show is recorded

65 **unconscious** (page 35)
in a condition similar to sleep in which you do not see, feel or think, usually because you are injured

94

66 **mellowed** – *to mellow* (page 37)
   if you *mellow*, or if something *mellows* you, you become gentler,
   wiser, and easier to talk to, especially because of age or experience

67 **compromise** – *to compromise* (page 37)
   to solve a problem or end an argument by accepting that you
   cannot have everything that you want

68 **desperate** (page 37)
   very worried and uncomfortable because you do not know how to
   deal with an unpleasant situation

69 **shut up** – *to shut up* (page 37)
   to stop talking or making a noise

70 **emotional support** (page 39)
   help and kindness that you give to someone who is having a
   difficult time

71 **live** (page 40)
   a *live* television or radio programme can be watched or listened to
   at the same time as it happens

72 **musical** (page 40)
   a play or film in which there are a lot of songs

73 **performance** (page 40)
   If you *perform* something, you do it in front of an audience in order
   to entertain them, for example by acting in a play or singing. The
   action of doing this is called a *performance*.

74 **set** (page 42)
   a stage or other place where a film or television programme is made
   or where a play is performed

75 **earpiece** (page 43)
   a small piece of electronic equipment that you put in your ear in
   order to listen to something, especially recorded music

76 **warm-up** (page 43)
   a short entertainment that is performed before the main
   performance of a concert or television show to make the audience
   relaxed and excited

77 **disaster** (page 43)
   something that is terrible or a failure

78 **trapped** (page 46)
   unable to change a bad situation or way of thinking

79 **stockings** (page 48)
   a piece of clothing worn on a woman's foot and leg, held up by
   suspenders – a piece of women's underwear that hangs down from a
   belt and is fastened to a stocking to hold it up

80 **obnoxious** (page 49)
very rude, offensive or unpleasant
81 **resignation** (page 54)
the act of leaving a job permanently. If you do this, you *resign*.
82 **marketing** (page 56)
the ways in which a company encourages people to buy its products
by deciding on price, type of customer and advertising policy
83 **trusted** – *to trust someone* (page 57)
to be confident that someone is honest, fair and reliable
84 **advance** (page 59)
a payment for work that is given before the work is complete
85 **maze** (page 60)
an arrangement of closely connected paths separated by tall bushes
or trees. The paths often do not lead anywhere, and you have to use
your memory and skill to get through
86 **blame** – *to blame someone or something* (page 60)
to say or think that someone or something is responsible for an
accident, problem or bad situation
87 **transform** – *to transform something* (page 61)
to make someone or something completely different, usually in a
way that makes them better or more attractive
88 **ruin** – *to ruin something* (page 61)
to destroy or severely damage something. Emma is saying that now
she won't be able to marry Dexter, but then she says that it is a
joke.
89 **pressure** (page 62)
a strong feeling of wanting or needing to do something. If you *give
in to pressure*, you do something you want to do, even though you
know that you shouldn't.
90 **menial work** (page 62)
work that is boring or dirty and is considered to be of low status
91 **broken up** – *to break up* (page 67)
if a relationship *breaks up*, it ends
92 **fortnight** (page 68)
a period of two weeks
93 **moved on** – *to move on from someone or something* (page 70)
to start to continue with your life after you have dealt successfully
with a bad experience
94 **delicatessen** (page 70)
a shop that sells food such as cooked meat, cheese and food from
other countries. This kind of shop is often simply called a *deli*.

95 **protested** – *to protest about something* (page 75)
to disagree strongly with something, often by making a formal
statement or taking action in public
96 **anniversary** (page 78)
a date that is an exact number of years after the date of an
important or special event
97 **Arthur's Seat** (page 80)
the top of a mountain in Edinburgh which has views of the city and
the countryside around it
98 **romantic** (page 82)
making you have feelings of love and excitement
99 **exhausted** – *to be exhausted* (page 84)
to be someone extremely tired and without energy

Useful Phrases

broadens the mind – *to broaden the mind* (page 7)
to help you understand the world and make you more able to accept other people's ideas and beliefs

Why on earth … ? (page 14)
used for emphasizing a question

earn some money on the side – *to do something on the side* (page 18)
if you do or have something *on the side*, you do or have it in addition to what is usual

go on a date – *to go on a date with someone* (page 18)
to spend time with someone who you are having or starting a sexual or romantic relationship with, for example at a restaurant or the cinema

wire you some money – *to wire some money to someone* (page 19)
to send money directly from one bank to another using an electronic system

I'll come straight to the point – *to come straight to the point* (page 21)
to stop talking about unimportant details and say what is most important

he took you for granted – *to take someone for granted* (page 38)
to expect someone to always be there and do things for you even when you do not show that you are grateful

in charge of – *to be in charge of something* (page 40)
if you are *in charge*, you have control over someone or something and are responsible for them

to settle his nerves – *to settle your nerves* (page 41)
to stop yourself from feeling nervous

I owe you an apology – *to owe someone an apology* (page 44)
to feel that you should say sorry to someone for doing something wrong or causing a problem

on top of the world (page 45)
in a very good mood because things are going well for you

with a good heart (page 54)
someone who has *a good heart* is a kind person

Sylvie was on his side – *to be on someone's side* (page 57)
to support someone, or remain loyal to them

getting rid of her – *to get rid of someone* (page 60)
to make someone go away because they are annoying, unpleasant or
not wanted

Exercises

Background Information

Read 'A Note About The Author' and 'A Note About The Story'.
Write T (True) or F (False).

1   David Nicholls went to an expensive school. __F__

2   He did a degree in English and Drama. _____

3   He was an actor for ten years. _____

4   He wrote dramas for TV and radio. _____

5   He has written three novels. _____

6   David Nicholls is married. _____

7   *One Day* is about difficulties in relationships. _____

8   The book is about one specific day in the past. _____

9   'Picaresque' novels tell a continuous story. _____

10 The novel tells us about society at that time. _____

11 The novel is set in the 1950s. _____

12 The book has been made into a film. _____

People in the Story

Write a name from the box next to the correct information below.

> Alison   Callum   Dexter   Emma   Ian   Jasmine
> Maddy   Phil   Stephen   Suki   Sylvie   Tilly

1 _____Alison_____ was Dexter's mother.

2 _____ had rich parents who lived in Oxfordshire.

3 _____ was born in Yorkshire.

4 _____ was Dexter's daughter.

5 _____ was the headteacher at the school where
Emma worked.

6 _____ was a successful TV presenter.

7 _____ was Emma's friend and flatmate.

8 _____ was Dexter's father.

9 _____ worked with Emma at a Tex-Mex restaurant.

10 _____ was Dexter's first wife.

11 _____ shared a flat with Dexter in Edinburgh.

12 _____ was Dexter's last girlfriend.

Events and Places in the Story

Match the events on the left to the places on the right.

1	Emma met Dexter at university.	a	Yorkshire
2	Dexter taught English as a foreign language.	b	Soho
3	Emma worked in a restaurant.	c	Walthamstow
4	Dexter met a TV producer while travelling.	d	Greece
5	Emma and Dexter swam naked in the sea.	e	Rome
6	Dexter visited his dying mother.	f	Chichester
7	Emma got a teaching job.	g	Richmond
8	Emma and Ian bought a flat together.	h	Highgate
9	Emma ended her friendship with Dexter.	i	Somerset
10	Dexter realized he was in love with Sylvie.	j	Paris
11	Dexter and Emma met for the first time after three years.	k	Leytonstone
12	Dexter lived with Sylvie and baby Jasmine.	l	Edinburgh
13	Dexter visited Emma and they started a relationship.	m	Oxfordshire
14	Dexter opened his own delicatessen.	n	India
15	Emma and Dexter went on holiday after deciding to get married.	o	Camden Town

Vocabulary: Describing character

Complete the gaps. Use each word in the box once.

> ambition   arrogant   emotional support   flirting   idiot
> mellow   monster   posh   sober   ~~socialist~~

1 Emma had strong opinions when she was at university. She was a
   ___*socialist*___ and believed in having an equal society.

2 Emma worked in a restaurant but had an _____ to be a
   writer.

3 When she got older, Emma's opinions became softer as she became
   more _____ .

4 Emma really helped Dexter after his mother died and gave him a lot
   of _____ .

5 Dexter was from a higher social class and Emma thought he was
   _____ .

6 Dexter believed he was better than other people and Emma thought
   he was _____ .

7 She said he was stupid and called him an _____ .

8 She didn't think he was cruel like a _____ .

9 Dexter spent most of his younger life talking to pretty women and
   _____ with them.

10 He was often drunk and was hardly ever _____ .

Vocabulary: Anagrams

Write the letters in the correct order to make the words from the story.

1	ECOMEVOR	*overcome*	to manage a problem successfully
2	TSRICPRWTREI		a person who writes the words for films and TV programmes
3	ARELENT		continuing forever or for a very long time
4	REDPENT		to make people think you are doing something or are something which you are not
5	PETUS		to make someone sad or angry
6	HIGS		to breathe out slowly making a soft sound
7	ASRCREHE		to study something in detail to find out new things
8	BOYE		to do what a law or someone tells you to do
9	MALEB		to say that a person is responsible for a bad situation
10	FARNSTORM		to make someone or something completely different
11	PERUSERS		a strong feeling of wanting or needing to do something
12	CEASEDLISTEN		a shop which sells fresh food (often meat and cheese)

Complete the gaps. Use six words from the table on page 104.

1 After many years, Dexter and Emma were finally able to
  overcome their problems.

2 Dexter had a .... in a fashionable part of north London.

3 Dexter thought that being a father would .... his life.

4 David Nicholls was a .... before he started to write novels.

5 Dexter often .... Emma by bringing his girlfriends to see her.

6 Emma made five rules for her and Dexter to .... on holiday.

7 Dexter said that he did not .... Emma for ending their
  friendship.

Word Focus

Write the words in the box into the correct column.

an advance   a chain   a gig   a manager   a musical   a performance
a presenter   a producer   a set   a television studio   marketing
menial work   resignation   stand-up comedy

Entertainment	Jobs and Business
a musical	*an advance*

105

Useful Phrases

Match a verb on the left with the words on the right to make a phrase from the book.

1	wire	a	in charge of something
2	go	b	the mind
3	take	c	a good heart
4	broaden	d	someone money
5	come	e	on a date
6	be	f	your nerves
7	owe	g	someone for granted
8	settle	h	rid of something / someone
9	have	i	straight to the point
10	get	j	someone an apology

Match the expressions above to their meanings below.

1 to send money electronically _1_

2 to expect someone's help or support but without showing you are grateful _____

3 to think that you need to say sorry to someone _____

4 to spend time with someone you are starting a relationship with _____

5 to do something to stop you feeling nervous _____

6 to be a good, kind person _____

7 to be the boss or to be responsible for something _____

8 to immediately give the most important information _____

9 to give you more experience of the world _____

10 to move something out of your life because it's not necessary for you anymore _____

Grammar: Present tenses

Use the verbs in brackets to complete Emma's diary using the present simple, present continuous or present perfect.

15th July 1990

> **Example:** I've been (go) to university and at the moment I'm working (work) in a Mexican restaurant in Camden town, which sells (sell) horrible food.

However, I (1) .... (meet) a nice man called Ian.
He (2) .... (do) stand-up comedy every week.
I (3) .... (still try) to get my poems published.

15th July 1994

I (4) .... (move) to Leytonstone and I (5) ....
(have) a job in a comprehensive school, where I (6) ....
(teach) English and Drama. Ian (7) .... (move) into my flat
and I think I (8) .... (love) him, but he (9) ....
(not like) Dexter. So, Dexter ... Well, his mother is very ill and he
(10) .... (drink) too much these days.

Grammar: *Wish*

Use the verbs in brackets to write the sentences using *wish* + past simple or *wish* + past perfect.

> **Example 1:** Dexter didn't send Emma the letter from India.
> Dexter *wishes he'd sent Emma the letter from India.*
> **Example 2:** Dexter's mother is dead.
> Dexter *wishes his mother wasn't / weren't dead.*

1 Dexter has a difficult life.
  Dexter ....

2 The newspapers wrote horrible things about Dexter.
  Dexter ....

3 Dexter's vodka bottle got mixed up with the water bottle.
  Dexter ....

4 Dexter's TV career wasn't successful.
  Dexter ....

5 Dexter waited a long time before going out with Emma.
  Dexter ....

6 Dexter is sad that Emma took her bicycle to meet him.
  Dexter ....

7 Maddy left Dexter alone on the night of Emma's first anniversary.
  Maddy ....

8 Maddy thinks that Dexter misses Emma a lot.
  Maddy ....

9 Maddy doesn't have any children of her own.
  Maddy ....

10 Dexter and Maddy want to live in a bigger house.
   Dexter and Maddy ....

Making Questions

Write questions for the answers given.

> **Example:**   Emma and Dexter met at Edinburgh University.
> *Where did Emma and Dexter meet?*

1   Dexter taught English in Rome.

2   On *The Bigger Picture*, Dexter interviewed actors and singers.

3   Emma taught English and Drama.

4   Emma ended her friendship with Dexter because she didn't like him anymore.

5   Dexter and Sylvie got divorced because Sylvie had started a relationship with Callum.

6   Dexter read Emma's book on the train to Paris.

7   Emma wrote her books in her flat.

8   Emma and Dexter argued because they couldn't have a baby.

9   On the first anniversary, Dexter went to a drinking club in Central London.

10   He spent the second anniversary alone.

11   He went to Edinburgh on the third anniversary.

12   Maddy is Dexter's girlfriend now.

Pronunciation: Word stress

Put the two-syllable words from the box into the correct column according to the main stress.

> advance   annoyed   ~~connect~~   ~~contact~~   cuddle   deserve
> despair   divorce   fascist   fortnight   obey   poison   pretend
> publish   selfish   slogan   sober   upset   victim

● ●	● ●
contact	connect

Put the three-syllable words from the box into the correct columns according to the main stress.

> ~~ambition~~   ~~arrogant~~   compromise   disaster   episode   eternal
> exhausted   graduate   idiot   manager   musical   nudity   offended
> performance   producer   scriptwriter   socialist   unconscious

● ● ●	● ● ●
arrogant	ambition

Visit the Macmillan Readers website at
www.macmillanenglish.com/readers

*to find **FREE resources** for use in class and for independent learning. Search our **online catalogue** to buy new Readers including **audio download** and **eBook** versions.*

Here's a taste of what's available:

For the classroom:

- **Tests** for every Reader to check understanding and monitor progress
- **Worksheets** for every Reader to explore language and themes
- **Listening worksheets** to practise extensive listening
- Worksheets to help prepare for the **FCE reading exam**

Additional resources for students and independent learners:

- An **online level test** to identify reading level
- **Author information sheets** to provide in-depth biographical information about our Readers authors
- **Self-study worksheets** to help track and record your reading which can be used with any Reader
- Use our **creative writing worksheets** to help you write short stories, poetry and biographies
- Write academic essays and literary criticism confidently with the help of our **academic writing worksheets**
- Have fun completing our **webquests** and **projects** and learn more about the Reader you are studying
- Go backstage and read **interviews** with **famous authors** and **actors**
- Discuss your favourite Readers at the **Book Corner Club**

Visit www.macmillanenglish.com/readers to find out more!

Published by Macmillan Heinemann ELT
Between Towns Road, Oxford OX4 3PP
A division of Macmillan Publishers Limited
Companies and representatives throughout the world
Heinemann is the registered trademark of Pearson Education, used under licence.

ISBN 978-0-230-42232-2
ISBN 978-0-230-42235-3 (with CD edition)

This version of *One Day* by David Nicholls was retold by
F H Cornish for Macmillan Readers.

First published 2012
Text, design and illustration © Macmillan Publishers Limited 2012

Designed by Carolyn Gibson
Illustrated by Bruce Emmett
Cover photograph by Alamy/Sergiy Serdyuk

Printed and bound in Thailand

without CD edition

2017	2016	2015	2014	2013	2012
10	9	8	7	6	5	4	3	2	1

with CD edition

2017	2016	2015	2014	2013	2012
10	9	8	7	6	5	4	3	2	1